First World War
and Army of Occupation
War Diary
France, Belgium and Germany

19 DIVISION
56 Infantry Brigade
Cheshire Regiment
9th Battalion
10 February 1918 - 28 February 1919

WO95/2079/1

The Naval & Military Press Ltd
www.nmarchive.com
Published in association with The National Archives

Published by

The Naval & Military Press Ltd

Unit 10 Ridgewood Industrial Park,

Uckfield, East Sussex,

TN22 5QE England

Tel: +44 (0) 1825 749494

www.naval-military-press.com

www.nmarchive.com

This diary has been reprinted in facsimile from the original. Any imperfections are inevitably reproduced and the quality may fall short of modern type and cartographic standards.

© Crown Copyright
Images reproduced by permission of The National Archives, London, England, 2015.

Contents

Document type	Place/Title	Date From	Date To
Heading	WO95/2079/1		
Heading	9th Bn Cheshire Regt Feb 1918-Feb 1919 From 58 Bde		
Heading	9th Head Regt War Diary		
War Diary	Front Line Trenches 34 (Sheet 57c)	01/07/1918	01/07/1918
War Diary	Hawes Camp Wes (P.18.d Sheet S/c)	02/07/1918	02/07/1918
War Diary	Hawes Camp East	03/07/1918	03/07/1918
War Diary	Hawes Camp East (Sheet 57c)	03/07/1918	05/07/1918
War Diary	Front Line Right Battn Sector	06/07/1918	09/07/1918
War Diary	Westwood Camp (Hawes Camp West)	10/02/1918	12/02/1918
War Diary	Front Line (Left Battn)	12/02/1918	14/02/1918
War Diary	Talavera Camp Barastre	15/02/1918	22/02/1918
War Diary	Bruce Huts Aveluy (Reft Map Lensil)	23/02/1918	23/02/1918
War Diary	Senlis (Ref Map Lensil)	24/02/1918	28/02/1918
War Diary	9th Battalion Cheshire Regiment March 1918		
War Diary	Senlis	01/03/1918	07/03/1918
War Diary	Beaulencourt N 24 b (Sheet 57c)	08/03/1918	21/03/1918
War Diary	Gaika Copse (1.36.d.9.0) Sheet 57 C	21/03/1918	21/03/1918
War Diary	Delsaux Farm (1.28a Sheet 57c)	22/03/1918	24/03/1918
War Diary	Bapaume	24/03/1918	24/03/1918
War Diary	Grevillers	25/03/1918	25/03/1918
War Diary	Grevillers (G.30 Sheet 57c)	25/03/1918	25/03/1918
War Diary	Irles Bucquoy Pusieux Souastre	26/03/1918	26/03/1918
War Diary	Achiet-Le-Petit	26/03/1918	26/03/1918
War Diary	Souastre	26/03/1918	26/03/1918
War Diary	Henu	26/03/1918	26/03/1918
War Diary	Sailly-Au-Bois	27/03/1918	28/03/1918
War Diary	Famechon (Lens II)	29/03/1918	29/03/1918
War Diary	Ramillies Camp	30/03/1918	31/03/1918
Miscellaneous	56th. Infantry Brigade No. B.M. 891	04/03/1918	04/03/1918
Miscellaneous	App 201	03/03/1918	03/03/1918
Miscellaneous	56th Infantry Brigade No. B.M. 916	05/03/1918	05/03/1918
Miscellaneous	56th Infantry Brigade No. B.M. 916/1	06/03/1918	06/03/1918
Miscellaneous	App I 203	05/03/1918	05/03/1918
Miscellaneous	56th Infantry Brigade No. B.M. 891/1	04/03/1918	04/03/1918
Miscellaneous	App I 204	06/03/1918	06/03/1918
Operation(al) Order(s)	56th. Infantry Brigade Order No. 113	06/03/1918	06/03/1918
Miscellaneous	56th. Infantry Brigade Administrative Instructions No. 8 (Issued With reference to Brigade Order No. 113)	06/03/1918	06/03/1918
Miscellaneous	Train Table		
Miscellaneous	Instructions With Reference To The Move By Rail		
Miscellaneous	Location Table Beaulencourt Area		
Operation(al) Order(s)	9th (S) Bn. Cheshire Regt Order No 3	06/03/1918	06/03/1918
Miscellaneous	56th Infantry Brigade No. B.M. 918 App I 207	05/03/1918	05/03/1918
Miscellaneous	56th Infantry Brigade No. B.M. 1057	14/03/1918	14/03/1918
Miscellaneous	56th Infantry Brigade No. B.M. 1113 App I 211	19/03/1918	19/03/1918
Miscellaneous	Tactical Exercise With Tanks. No. 3.		
Operation(al) Order(s)	56th Infantry Brigade Order No. 114 App I 212	20/03/1918	20/03/1918
Miscellaneous	Table of Reliefs.-Appendix to 58th Inf. Bde. Order No. 114	20/03/1918	20/03/1918
Miscellaneous	A Form Messages And Signals.	20/03/1918	20/03/1918

Type	Description	Date 1	Date 2
Map	Right Bde. Dispositions	20/03/1918	20/03/1918
Miscellaneous	C Form Messages And Signals.		
Miscellaneous	Appendix J 213 (a)		
Miscellaneous	A Form Messages And Signals. App J 214	21/03/1918	21/03/1918
Miscellaneous		21/03/1918	21/03/1918
Miscellaneous	A Form Messages And Signals. App J 215	21/03/1918	21/03/1918
Operation(al) Order(s)	56th Infantry Brigade Order No. 115 App J 216	21/03/1918	21/03/1918
Map			
Miscellaneous	A Form Messages And Signals. App J 217	21/03/1918	21/03/1918
Miscellaneous	C Form Messages And Signals. App J 218	21/03/1918	21/03/1918
Miscellaneous	56th Infantry Brigade No. B.M. 1157 App J 219	23/03/1918	23/03/1918
Miscellaneous	56th Infantry Brigade No. B.M. 662/Q. App J 220	22/03/1918	22/03/1918
Miscellaneous	A Form Messages And Signals. App J 221	23/03/1918	23/03/1918
Miscellaneous	B Form Messages And Signals. App J 222	23/03/1918	23/03/1918
Miscellaneous	56th Infantry Brigade No. 343/S. App J 223	23/03/1918	23/03/1918
Miscellaneous	A Form Messages And Signals. App J 224	24/03/1918	24/03/1918
Miscellaneous	A Form Messages And Signals.	24/03/1918	24/03/1918
Miscellaneous	A Form Messages And Signals.		
Miscellaneous	To A B C D Corp App J 225		
Miscellaneous	A Form Messages And Signals. App J 226	26/03/1918	26/03/1918
Miscellaneous	A Form Messages And Signals.		
Miscellaneous	A Form Messages And Signals. App J 227	27/03/1918	27/03/1918
Miscellaneous	A Form Messages And Signals.		
Operation(al) Order(s)	56th. Infantry Brigade Order No. 116 App J 228	28/03/1918	28/03/1918
Miscellaneous	56th. Infantry Brigade No. B.M. 1177	28/03/1918	28/03/1918
Miscellaneous	March Table.		
Operation(al) Order(s)	9th Bov Cheshire Regt Order No 4	28/03/1918	28/03/1918
Miscellaneous	56th Infantry Brigade No. B.M.	28/03/1918	28/03/1918
Operation(al) Order(s)	56th Infantry Brigade Order No. 117	28/03/1918	28/03/1918
Miscellaneous	March Table		
Miscellaneous	Entraining Table		
Miscellaneous	Table of personnel to be detailed by Units at entraining and detraining stations.		
Operation(al) Order(s)	56th Infantry Brigade No. O.O. 117/1	29/03/1918	29/03/1918
Miscellaneous	A Form Messages And Signals.	29/03/1918	29/03/1918
Heading	1/9th Battalion The Cheshire Regiment April 1918		
War Diary	Ramillies Camp (N. 27.b.0.5) Sheet	01/04/1918	06/04/1918
War Diary	T.5. Central (Sheet 28 S.W)	07/04/1918	08/04/1918
War Diary	Rossignol Camp (N.21.b.9.1)	09/04/1918	10/04/1918
War Diary	Nieppe (B.15.116 Sheet 36)	10/04/1918	10/04/1918
War Diary	Courte Rue (B.10. Sheet 36)	11/04/1918	11/04/1918
War Diary	Court Rue (B.10 Sheet 36)	11/04/1918	11/04/1918
War Diary	Camperwisse Farm (B.3 Sheet 36)	11/04/1918	12/04/1918
War Diary	Lampernisse	12/04/1918	12/04/1918
War Diary	Ravelsburg	13/04/1918	14/04/1918
War Diary	Koudokot	15/04/1918	15/04/1918
War Diary	Kemmel Defences	16/04/1918	18/04/1918
War Diary	Kemmel	18/04/1918	19/04/1918
War Diary	Wippenhoek	20/04/1918	21/04/1918
War Diary	Tunnellers Camp (F. 27a Sheet 27)	22/04/1918	25/04/1918
War Diary	Ouderdom	26/04/1918	30/04/1918
Operation(al) Order(s)	9th Bn. Cheshire Regiment Order No. 5	31/03/1918	31/03/1918
Miscellaneous	Headquarters 56th Bn Battalion Arrived In Gable Camp		
Operation(al) Order(s)	9th (S) Bn. Cheshire Regiment Order No. 6	07/04/1918	07/04/1918
Miscellaneous	Urgent.	07/04/1918	07/04/1918
Miscellaneous	(Sgd) B. in Thurn, Capt. Bde. Major		

Type	Description	Start	End
Miscellaneous	56th Infantry Brigade S.C./1.	18/04/1918	18/04/1918
Miscellaneous	Warning Order	20/04/1918	20/04/1918
Miscellaneous	Reference Map Sheet 27	23/04/1918	23/04/1918
War Diary	Duoerdom G24 (Sheet 28)	01/05/1918	01/05/1918
War Diary	Dickebusch Lake	02/05/1918	04/05/1918
War Diary	G16.b.48. (Sheet 28)	05/05/1918	05/05/1918
War Diary	L.8.c.3.6 (Sheet 27)	06/05/1918	12/05/1918
War Diary	H23.d.7.7	12/05/1918	12/05/1918
War Diary	Z8.c.3.6	13/05/1918	13/05/1918
War Diary	H.23.a.77 (Sheet 27)	14/05/1918	18/05/1918
War Diary	La Chaussee	18/05/1918	29/05/1918
War Diary	Sarcy	29/05/1918	30/05/1918
War Diary	South of Sarcy	31/05/1918	31/05/1918
War Diary	Near Chambrecy	01/06/1918	03/06/1918
War Diary	Montagne De Blieny	03/06/1918	07/06/1918
War Diary	Bois de Courton	07/06/1918	09/06/1918
War Diary	Foret de Reims	09/06/1918	20/06/1918
War Diary	Le Mesnil	20/06/1918	21/06/1918
War Diary	Reuves	21/06/1918	24/06/1918
War Diary	Broussy-Le-Petit	25/06/1918	30/06/1918
War Diary	Bannes	30/06/1918	30/06/1918
War Diary	Bannes Ref Map Chalons	01/07/1918	01/07/1918
War Diary	Planques Ref Map Lens II	02/07/1918	04/07/1918
War Diary	Wicquinghem Ref Map Calais 13	05/07/1918	09/07/1918
War Diary	Wicquinghem	10/07/1918	13/07/1918
War Diary	Ames Ref Map	14/07/1918	14/07/1918
War Diary	Hazebrouck 5a	15/07/1918	23/07/1918
War Diary	Ames	24/07/1918	05/08/1918
War Diary	Locon Sector	06/08/1918	09/08/1918
War Diary	Support Trenches Locon Sector	10/08/1918	15/08/1918
War Diary	Front Line Trenches Locon Sector (Ref Map Sheet 36 SE)	16/08/1918	21/08/1918
War Diary	Support Trenches	22/08/1918	31/08/1918
War Diary	Annezin	01/09/1918	02/09/1918
War Diary	Locon	03/09/1918	05/09/1918
War Diary	Richbourg	06/09/1918	16/09/1918
War Diary	La Motte	17/09/1918	22/09/1918
War Diary	Lacouture	23/09/1918	26/09/1918
War Diary	Neuve Chapelle	26/09/1918	02/10/1918
War Diary	Raimbert	03/10/1918	04/10/1918
War Diary	Couturelle	05/10/1918	07/10/1918
War Diary	Graincourt	08/10/1918	09/10/1918
War Diary	Proville	10/10/1918	17/10/1918
War Diary	Avenes Lez Aubert	17/10/1918	19/10/1918
War Diary	St Aubert	19/10/1918	23/10/1918
War Diary	Cagnoncles	24/10/1918	31/10/1918
Operation(al) Order(s)	9th Bn Cheshire Regiment. Operation Order No. 132.	04/10/1918	04/10/1918
Operation(al) Order(s)	56th Infantry Brigade Operation Order No. 158	03/10/1918	03/10/1918
Operation(al) Order(s)	56th Infantry Brigade Operation Order No. 159	06/10/1918	06/10/1918
Operation(al) Order(s)	56th Infantry Brigade Operation Order No. 162	22/10/1918	22/10/1918
War Diary	Cagnoncles	01/11/1918	01/11/1918
War Diary	Sommaing	02/11/1918	02/11/1918
War Diary	Maresches	03/11/1918	09/11/1918
War Diary	Taisnieres	10/11/1918	14/11/1918
War Diary	Sommaing	15/11/1918	15/11/1918
War Diary	Rieux	16/11/1918	25/11/1918

War Diary	Fauberg De Paris	25/11/1918	28/11/1918
War Diary	Naours	28/11/1918	30/11/1918
Operation(al) Order(s)	56th Infantry Brigade Operation Order No. 165	03/11/1918	03/11/1918
Miscellaneous	56th Infantry Brigade Administrative Instructions No. 36	03/11/1918	03/11/1918
Operation(al) Order(s)	56th Infantry Brigade Operation Order No. 167	09/11/1918	09/11/1918
Operation(al) Order(s)	56th Infantry Brigade Operation Order No. 168	13/11/1918	13/11/1918
Operation(al) Order(s)	56th Infantry Brigade Operation Order No. 169	14/11/1918	14/11/1918
Miscellaneous	Headquarters, 56th Infantry Brigade.	17/11/1918	17/11/1918
War Diary	Naours	01/12/1918	11/12/1918
War Diary	Villers L'Hopital	12/12/1918	28/02/1919

WO 95/2079/1

19TH DIVISION
56TH INFY BDE

9TH BN CHESHIRE REGT
FEB 1918-FEB 1919

From 58 BDE

To 1 DIV (RHINE ARMY)

Cover for Documents.

Nature of Enclosures.

WAR DIARY

Notes, or Letters written.

9th Cheshire Regt.

Feb 1918
Feb 1919

9/C/19

9th Cheshire Regt.

Army Form W.3021.

WAR DIARY or INTELLIGENCE SUMMARY.

Army Form C. 2118.

Place	Date	Hour	Summary of Events and Information	Remarks and references to Appendices
FRONT LINE Linchuy Level (sheet 27c)	1918 July 1		The day passed without incident - visibility was low and observation impossible except on the front line area. Circumference with Brigade Orders No 228 (App J 742) and Battn Orders No 463 (App J 743) the Battn was relieved by the 1/4 EAST LANCS. The night was very dark but the relief was carried out without hindrance and was completed by 9.15 p.m., the Battalion travelling back 6 HAWKES CAMP WEST by motor lorries till Companies and H.Q. were billeted by 11.15 p.m. and a hot meal served to the men. The Battalion was	App J 741 App J 742 App J 743
HAWKES CAMP WEST (sheet 27c)	2		now in Reserve under the H.Q. of the 57th Inf. Brigade. The morning was spent in cleaning up. In the afternoon in accordance with Para 3 Brigade Order No 238 the Battalion moved from HAWKES CAMP (App J 744(a)) WEST to H.Q. WES CAMP EAST, billeting was completed by 4.40 p.m. 57th Inf. Brigade relieved 58th Brigade H.Q. in Bro Fork over command for Tactical purposes of the Battalion in reserve (App J 746). Orders were received that the reorganisation of the Battalion of the Division, on a three	App J 744(a) App J 745 App J 746
" EAST	3		Battalion basis would begin on July 4th (App J 747). Lieut. F.G. FOX reported on arrival	App J 747

WAR DIARY
OR
INTELLIGENCE SUMMARY.
(Erase heading not required.)

Army Form C. 2118.

Place	Date	Hour	Summary of Events and Information	Remarks and references to Appendices
HAWKES CAMP EAST (Sh4 37c)	1918 Feby 3		Working parties were supplied. Baths were also used.	App J 178
	4		The same units. 9th VERITY, A. RILEY. W. N. STUBBS, J. W. BROOKS, Lt. STODDARD "100 ORS Ply. arrived.	
	5		In accordance with instructions contained in 58th Bde Order No 229 (App J 148 a) and Batln. Order No 2 (App J 179 b) The Battalion moved up to relief of the 9th R.W.Fusiliers and marched out of Camp at 4.15 p.m. and entrained on the light railway at P.18.c.11 Train moved off at 4.30 p.m. and the Battalion detrained at TRESCAULT and proceeded by foot thence to the front line. Relief was complete by 11 p.m. disposition of companies being as stated in Batln Orders (App J 179 b) and Disposition Report (J 179 c)	App J 148 a App J 179 (b) App J 179 c
FRONT LINE Right Centre Section	6		A Jongale wire was received just after midnight warning The Battalion that a hostile raid appeared possible on the Divisional front and special vigilance was ordered. The morning passed without incident however. The usual protective patrols having nothing to report.	App J 180 App J 181

Army Form C. 2118.

WAR DIARY
or
INTELLIGENCE SUMMARY.
(Erase heading not required.)

Instructions regarding War Diaries and Intelligence Summaries are contained in F. S. Regs., Part II. and the Staff Manual respectively. Title pages will be prepared in manuscript.

Place	Date	Hour	Summary of Events and Information	Remarks and references to Appendices
Front Line Right Battn Sector	1918 Feby 7		Patrols went out and reconnoitred enemy positions from this day. The two strongpoints continous forms part of the 58th Inf. Brigade.	App J183 App J183
	8		Patrols were out in the early morning. 58th Strongpoints took over Command of the right subsector from the 58th Inf. Brigade	App J184 App J185
	9		Naval patrols went out in the morning. In accordance with 58th Inf Brigade Order No 101 (App J.197) and Battn Order (App J187a) the Battalion was relieved by the 8 Bn H Staff. Relief was complete by 10.35 p.m (App J187b) and the Battalion moved back into billets	App J186 App J187
WESTWOOD CAMP (17th W/125 Camp WEST)	10		CAMP WEST, which it reached by 2.0 a.m (App J187c). Lewis guns for anti-aircraft defence were detailed in accordance with Bde. Orders (App J188) The morning was spent in rest. The remainder of the day in cleaning up. 117 O.R. reinforcement arrived	App J188
	11		Inspections, working parties and baths. 52 O.R. reinforcement arrived	
	12		On the evening of the 12th, in accordance with 58th Inf Bde Order No 107 and Battn Orders No 5 (App J189) the Battalion moved up and relieved the 9th Bn Fusiliers in the left Battn Front, taking over a slightly	App J189

WAR DIARY
or
INTELLIGENCE SUMMARY.
(Erase heading not required.)

Army Form C. 2118.

Instructions regarding War Diaries and Intelligence Summaries are contained in F. S. Regs., Part II. and the Staff Manual respectively. Title pages will be prepared in manuscript.

Place	Date	Hour	Summary of Events and Information	Remarks and references to Appendices
FRONT LINE (Left Battn.)	1918 Feb. 12		entered front (extended to the right. App J119.6. Dispositions as stated on App. J190. Relief was completed by 9.20 pm (App J119c). The left front	J119.c J190
	13		Company was subjected to rather heavy French mortaring during the early hours of the morning, but no casualties were suffered.	App J91
	14		The day passed without incident. In accordance with 56th Inf Brigade Order No 107 and Batn Orders A2/52 (App J93) the battalion was relieved by the DRAKE Bn of the R.N.D. and moved back by light railway to TALAVERA Camp near BARASTRE. The Transport and G.N. Stores moved in	App J92 App J93 App J94
TALAVERA CAMP BARASTRE	15		accordance with Brigade Administrative Instructions No 1 and the complete Battalion was billeted in camp by 5.15 a.m.	
	16		Rest and cleaning up.	
	17		Inspections and Church Parades.	
	18		Training. 86 O.R. Reinforcements arrived.	
	19		do	
	20		do	

Army Form C. 2118.

WAR DIARY
or
INTELLIGENCE SUMMARY.
(Erase heading not required.)

Instructions regarding War Diaries and Intelligence Summaries are contained in F. S. Regs., Part II. and the Staff Manual respectively. Title pages will be prepared in manuscript.

Place	Date	Hour	Summary of Events and Information	Remarks and references to Appendices
TALAVERA CAMP BAMASTRE	1918 Feby 21		A warning order was received that the Brigade would move to an area about MERICOURT and an advance party was despatched at 5 p.m. At 9.30 p.m. orders were received that the Brigade would move by route march (App J196). At 11 p.m. previous orders cancelled (App J197) and warning issued that the Brigade would move by train.	App J196 App J197
	22		In accordance with Brigade Order No. 111 (App J198a) and Batt. Order No. 1 (App J198b) the Battalion entrained at ROCQUIGNY at 11 a.m. and arrived at ALBERT about 2.30 p.m. The Battalion was billeted in huts, this was completed by 5.15 p.m. the transport having arrived by road arrived by 7.30 p.m.	App J198 App J198
BRUCE HUTS ANZUY R.I.WAR LENS W.	23		The Battalion moved by march route from ANZUY to SENLIS where the Battalion was billeted in huts billets by 12.40 p.m. (App J199. This was the first time the Battalion had been billeted in an inhabited village since leaving EBBLINGHEN on December 8th 1917. Quartermaster Hon Lt W.R. Singer reported his arrival	App J199

A6945 Wt. W14422/M1160 350,000 12/16 D. D. & L. Forms/C/2118/14.

Army Form C. 2118.

WAR DIARY
or
INTELLIGENCE SUMMARY.
(Erase heading not required.)

Instructions regarding War Diaries and Intelligence Summaries are contained in F. S. Regs., Part II. and the Staff Manual respectively. Title pages will be prepared in manuscript.

Place	Date	Hour	Summary of Events and Information	Remarks and references to Appendices
SZNGIS	1917 Feb 24		Church Parade.	
(Willow Trench)	25		Training	
	26		Training	
	27		Training	
	28		Training. Lt Colonel JA Southey, proceeded to England for a six months tour of duty.	

E. Fulton. Major
Commanding 9th Cheshire Regt.

19th Division.
56th Infantry Brigade.

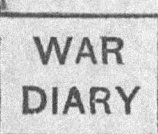

9th BATTALION

CHESHIRE REGIMENT

MARCH 1918

WAR DIARY
or
INTELLIGENCE SUMMARY.
(Erase heading not required.)

Army Form C. 2118.

1/Ches. R

Instructions regarding War Diaries and Intelligence Summaries are contained in F. S. Regs., Part II. and the Staff Manual respectively. Title pages will be prepared in manuscript.

Place	Date	Hour	Summary of Events and Information	Remarks and references to Appendices
SENLIS	1918 March 1		Training.	
	2		Training.	
	3		Training.	
	4		The relief of the 17th Division by the 19th Division was temporarily postponed but notice was received that the Battalion would relieve the 4th Border Regt when the relief takes place.	App S 300
			Training	
	5		Reconnoitring Parties visited the New Sector, proceeding by bus to the road junction S of HERMIES another by march route to junction of the road and railway at S.30.d.05.90 Reffrap Se.	App S 301
	6		The Corps' Chemical Adviser gave a demonstration of new gas projectors. Reconnoitring Parties again visited the new Sector as yesterday. Training	App S 302 App S 303
	7		The Brigade marched to BEAULENCOURT area, taking over the camp from the 5th Inf Brigade. The Battalion occupying the camp at N.24.b.3.0. (ref Map 5C vacated by the 8th Bn York Regt. The recent thaw made dry marching route to AVELUY and by train to BAPAUME. We returned via trench route from BAPAUME to BEAULENCOURT arriving in Camp at 1 pm.	App S 304 App S 305

Army Form C. 2118.

WAR DIARY
or
INTELLIGENCE SUMMARY.
(Erase heading not required.)

Instructions regarding War Diaries and Intelligence Summaries are contained in F. S. Regs., Part II. and the Staff Manual respectively. Title pages will be prepared in manuscript.

Place	Date	Hour	Summary of Events and Information	Remarks and references to Appendices
BEAULENCOURT N 24 L (Sh 57c)	1918 March 8		Training. A street reconnaissance of HERMIES was carried out	App J.207
	9		A Working Party of 7 Officers and 300 O.R. was found for work in the Battle Zone near TRESCAULT	App J.206
			From this date Orders detailing the Brigade's action in the event of Hostile Attack were received and special reconnoitring parties visited the forward areas. All these details were referred to companies and explained to all officers and NCOs. Training. I.O.R. reinforcement arrived. Interviewed by Brigade attack. Day carried out	App J.207
	10		Training	" "
	11		Training	
	12		A Working Party of 5 Officers and 300 O.R. was found for work in the Battle Zone near TRESCAULT	App J.208
	13		Training	
	14		Training	
	15		A working Party of 5 Officers and 300 O.R. was found for work in the Battle Zone near TRESCAULT	App J.209
	16		Training	
	17		A working party of 5 Officers and 300 O.R. was found for work in the Battle Zone near TRESCAULT	App J.210

WAR DIARY
or
INTELLIGENCE SUMMARY.
(Erase heading not required.)

Army Form C. 2118.

Place	Date	Hour	Summary of Events and Information	Remarks and references to Appendices
BEAULENCOURT (N.24.b Sheet 57c)	1918 March 17		Training	
"	18		Training	
"	19		A Tactical exercise with tanks was carried out. the Batt. forming trg details	App 7211
"	20		Order for the relief of the 52nd Inf. Brigade by the 56th Inf. Brigade on the night of the 23rd/24th March were received. O.O.R.I. arrived.	App 7212
"	20		A warning was received from Brigade that the expected enemy attack would take place on the following morning (the 21st) according to statements of captured enemy officers and men.	
"	21	5am	The sounds of heavy barrage fire were heard and the back areas were shelled by enemy H.V. guns. A stand to was accordingly ordered and at 5.35 a.m. war order stores kit was received from Appx.	App 7213
			Brigade, and all preparations were made for the move to camp in accordance with Brigade and Battalion Instructions.	App 7210
			The names of Offrs. who were to be left in reserve are shown on App.1. J 2/3(a) - 5 22 O.R who the fighting strength were drawn for the move to Camp, was 13 men.	App 7211 and the App 7214
			Battalion moved off to HARRICK CAMP at 11.10 p.m. Little equipment, bombs, additional S.B.R. tools, etc. were being issued to the Battalion.	App 7215
			11.15pm. On the order "move" move to Camp the 7th line transport moved with the Battalion the rest remaining at BEAULENCOURT.	

WAR DIARY or INTELLIGENCE SUMMARY.

Army Form C. 2118.

(Erase heading not required.)

Place	Date	Hour	Summary of Events and Information	Remarks and references to Appendices
GRANGE COPSE Nh. 1911 (I.30.d.95) (Sheet 57c)	21 April	4 p.m.	At 4 p.m. Orders were issued for the Battalion to move up to GRAIN COPSE (Ref. Map Sheet 57c) with the remainder of the Brigade in reserve which launched a counter attack against DOIGNIES. The move commenced at 4.15 pm. to the 5th Inf. Brigade. App to 57c.	App J215 J216
			Move was completed by 8.30 p.m. the Battalion being on the SE edge of the Copse. At 11 p.m. a warning was received that the Brigade would move Northwards to occupy positions of the GREEN LINE in I.21.b. and I.21.c. 12/7 Sheet 57c. at 11.45 a.m. at 1.30 am. Orders were received to rendezvous at DENSAUX FARM and the Battalion	App J217 App J218
DELSAUX FARM (I.27.a) (Sheet 57c)	22		moved off at 11.15 am and march ended near country to the point which was reached at 1.15 a.m. Dispositions (each with a Platoon in support of "B" Coy) "D" Coy being on the right, "B" in the centre, and "C" on the left. I.28 "A" Coy in support. Battalion frontage was the French line from I.27.d.53 The French was central to I.21.c.b to deposit. Coy being at I.27.b.53. 2.19.A. Grenadier etc captured and decided and attacks with 2.19.A. Grenadier etc from the dump which had been formed at I.28.a.O.L.	App J219 App J220
			Enemy aircraft was very active during the day flying in	

WAR DIARY
or
INTELLIGENCE SUMMARY.
(Erase heading not required.)

Army Form C. 2118.

Place	Date	Hour	Summary of Events and Information	Remarks and references to Appendices
BEISSEUX FARM	1918 March 22		dangerous and at low altitudes the day was clear, fine and visibility was very good. There was desultory shelling by the enemy with shrapnel + H.V. guns. The night passed quietly without incident. The first line transport returned to BEAUMENCOURT. 3rd O.R. killed and	
"	23		Battalion H.Q. moved by order from Brigade to dug outs at IZEL. Central Enemy shelling showed an increase both on the Battalion front trenches and roads. "Camp 1" on rear of Division PDH was established with South Staffs of the 6th Brigade on the Battalion right flank about I.28. Central. 3rd M.N. Staffs of our own Brigade were on the left. Towards evening the shelling became heavy but the night itself passed quietly. A warning was received that the enemy would attack on the Battalion frontage	App. 221 App. 222 App. 223
			and all "Counter preparations" were arranged. At 5.20pm instructions were received that all stores of value except those to be carried on the 2 baggage waggons were to be sent by motor lorry to POZIERES. Two lorries to make two journeys were allotted to the Battalion for this purpose. The transport and depot received orders at 8pm to move to GREVILLERS and were clear of BEAUMENCOURT by 3am 24 inst.	App. 222

WAR DIARY
or
INTELLIGENCE SUMMARY.

(Erase heading not required.)

Army Form C. 2118.

Instructions regarding War Diaries and Intelligence Summaries are contained in F. S. Regs., Part II. and the Staff Manual respectively. Title pages will be prepared in manuscript.

Place	Date	Hour	Summary of Events and Information	Remarks and references to Appendices
DELSAUX FARM	1918 March 24th		During the early hours of the morning our right company which was at DELSAUX farm Hill and contributed to advance of the Queens Essex led forces on reference point to the 9th BERCH who were now on our left front in the station copse of DELCNY. The Ability club carried out the counter preparation at 5am and 6-15am the troops holding DELCNY and to prevent front were however compelled by the heavy to withdraw. This later a real troop expected by the battalion held its ground knowing that at 7-30am later times however seen into defensive positions. At 9am the enemy put down a very heavy barrage on the battle front which lasted until 10:45am when an attack was delivered in mass. The latter was pressed up part of our front line breached but companies quickly reorganised to the support line and assisted by D Co, delivered a counter attack. The two Co by Captain A.D. MILNER and F.R. PARKER and ??? splendidly carried out — resulting in the re-taking of the lost trench and inflicting heavy casualties on the enemy. It was obvious that the enemy had suffered heavy casualties during his own attack. From 11am/2pm Lewis guns and rifle fire prepared orders were received for a withdrawal to the	App ???

WAR DIARY
or
INTELLIGENCE SUMMARY.

Army Form C. 2118.

Place	Date	Hour	Summary of Events and Information	Remarks and references to Appendices
DELSAUX FARM	1918 March 24th		Serval of the Brigade on to right going sound. There was found went to conference	App. 1/225
		At 2 pm	Definite orders were received that the 92nd Brigade's counter to withdraw and that the batts were to conform, but the battalion did not withdraw to H.26.a. (Sheet 57c)	
		However at 2 pm	the Brigadier ordered companies the right company there being about 6-40 and there was no opportunity of passing Company to the line who withdrew what forces it had to supervise assembling of the swing getting on the Enemies right flank	
BAPAUME			The 56th Brigade after withdrawal took up a line in H.34 & 35 in front of BAPAUME (Sheet 57c) and not believed as stated in the orders (App. 1/224). The battalion was here reinforced by 3 # officers (Captain MARTIN - Capt J.B. GRIFFITHS - ?Lieut E.C. FOX) and 83 O/R – rifles personnel from the transport lines – and dug in an are line from H.34.c.0.5 to H.34.c.85. At 5.30 pm orders were received to move back into the old German system in H.32.a. This was duly carried out and the battalion took up positions defending to S. of BAPAUME from attack of the LE TRANSLOY – BAPAUME Road. "B" & "C" Coys being in H.33.d. and "A" & "C" Coys in H.32.d. The battalion reorganised whilst here and C.O. C.M. in accordance with verbal orders received moved back to positions	

A6945 Wt. W14422/M1160 350,000 12/16 D.D.&L. Forms/C/2118/14.

WAR DIARY or INTELLIGENCE SUMMARY

Army Form C. 2118.

Place	Date	Hour	Summary of Events and Information	Remarks and references to Appendices
	1918 March 24		South of GREVILLERS (in support to K.S.L.I. in the front line) in G.36.a facing S.E.	
			The move was completed by 2 a.m. 25th March. In the march the following Cas- walties were sustained during the fighting of the 24th: killed in action – Capt. R.D.MILNER. Wounded – Capt. F.H.PARKER, Lieut. J.R.MALLALIEU, A.C.W. BENETT-DAMPIER, 2nd Lieut. N.CARRUTHERS, J.W.BROOKS, H.M.OWEN, W.M.STUBBS. Missing 2nd Lieut R.S.WELCH. At 9 p.m. the transport and quartermaster's stores were ordered to move to TREES. Numerous stragglers were collected by the Transport and returned to the battalion returns which were rendered about 10 p.m. in H.32.d (Sheet 57c).	
GREVILLERS 25			At 5 a.m. a reconnaissance of the positions occupied (GREVILLERS was carried out by the Commanding Officer and, in conjunction with the O.C. of N. Staffs ½/4th R.S.L.I. it was decided to take up final positions (on the left of the 5th N. Staffs Divn) in G.36.a and a third feeling patrol had been a gap to the line. There dis- positions were "D" Coy on the left - "C" Coy to the centre - "B" Coy on the right "A" Coy her in support and to the right & H.Q. were in rear of "A" and his 1 officer and 30 O.R. of the T.M. Battery attacked battn guard H.Q. entrenched at	

WAR DIARY
or
INTELLIGENCE SUMMARY.
(Erase heading not required.)

Army Form C. 2118.

Place	Date	Hour	Summary of Events and Information	Remarks and references to Appendices
GREVILLERS (G.30., 57c.)	1916 March 25th		moved to protect the right flank and obtain touch with the 51st Division on the right. At 9am the attack on the first line appeared to have commenced and by 12 noon the enemy was seen preparing to his attack on the battalion position. He suddenly broke forward under cover of M.G. and shrapnel fire under cover but was made by our troops on the main road in T.31.a and G.30.a. The troops at the Cutting had belonging to the Brigade on our left was withdrawn through GREVILLERS and the enemy was found possession of the high ground about G.36.b.5.0. 3 sections of M.G.'s of the 19th M.G. Batt. has taken up positions in the battalion support line and, together with M.G.s retaliated in LOUPART WOOD in G.34.b (Sheet 57c) inflicted heavy casualties on the enemy as he endeavoured to force large numbers of troops through over this high ground in G.36.b.5.0.	

Place	Date	Hour	Summary of Events and Information	Remarks and references to Appendices
GREVILLERS	1917 March 25		He was however able to establish M.G's at this point and with them enfiladed the Battalion's position. By 1.30pm enemy masses were able to approach the trenches and prepare for a heavy assault. The front companies were consequently withdrawn through the supports under cover of rifle fire and of M.G. fire from LOUPART WOOD in G.34 and 28. This latter fire proved most effective and inflicted very heavy casualties on the enemy who was seen to fall in large numbers. When the foremost enemy troops were beginning to swarm into the Battalion's support position, the remaining Companies withdrew under cover of small rear guards and formed up on the crest of the rise (about G.33.c.9.0) W. of LOUPART WOOD. From here the battalion in conjunction with the rest of the Brigade withdrew to the high ground in T.26.b. where fresh positions were taken up. Commanding the slopes down from LOUPART WOOD to IRLES. From this position fire was maintained on the enemy as he advanced down	

WAR DIARY or INTELLIGENCE SUMMARY

Army Form C. 2118.

Place	Date	Hour	Summary of Events and Information	Remarks and references to Appendices
	1918 March 25		the slopes through G.28, C.12.7.A+C. and round the valley from G.33 Central. Having been able to fight his way through in the low ground on the battalion right, the enemy was able to enfilade the Brigade positions from the direction of MIRAUMONT. In conjunction with troops on the left flank, the Brigade withdrew two the 62nd Division to positions in rear (the 63rd Div) on a new support line S.E. of MICHET-LE-PETIT, which were reached about 7 p.m. Capt J.H. GRIFFITHS and Lieuts. GRAY, KCFOX wounded in action, and 2nd Lt. HENRY missing (made his own dress of wound) Officer Casualties during the day. The Transport and Depot arrived at IRLES about 10 a.m.	
IRLES BUCQUOY PUSIEUX			and proceed to BUCQUOY. At 3.30 p.m. the Transport and Depot received orders to proceed to PUSIEUX, at 7.30 p.m. orders to move	
			to SOUASTRE were received and the Depot arrived in SOUASTRE	
SOUASTRE	26		about 2 a.m.	

WAR DIARY
of
INTELLIGENCE SUMMARY.
(Erase heading not required.)

Army Form C. 2118.

Place	Date	Hour	Summary of Events and Information	Remarks and references to Appendices
ACHIET-LE-PETIT	1918 March 25	5 a.m.	At 5 a.m. Verbal orders were received that the 19th Division would rendezvous W of BUCQUOY and the Battalion moved off at 5.15 a.m. On arrival at BUCQUOY information was obtained that the Division was re-organising at PORMIER, and the Battalion accordingly marched here and arrived about 12.30 p.m. A halt was made at HANNESCAMPS and a meal of dry rations and hot tea was served. Food was again supplied at PORMIER and the Battalion moved up to FONQUEVILLERS to the divisional sector of the front, where the 56th Brigade was to take up positions in reserve on relief of the Division but the 4th Australian Division, the Brigade Hd quarters at HEBUTERNE. On the evening of the 25th March and the 75th reports it appeared that at FONQUEVILLERS when the men were into reserve took place, bullets on valley 14-8708 men allotted to the territorial and were occupied by 9 p.m. A post for the purpose of giving alarm was put out on the road N.E. of SAILLY and commanding the approaches from HEBUTERNE.	App. S226
SOUASTRE		2 a.m.	The cooker arrived. Cooks were ordered to proceed to HEBUTERNE with rations for consumption today. At 9 a.m. Further orders	

WAR DIARY or INTELLIGENCE SUMMARY

Army Form C. 2118.

Instructions regarding War Diaries and Intelligence Summaries are contained in F. S. Regs., Part II. and the Staff Manual respectively. Title pages will be prepared in manuscript.

Place	Date 1918 March	Hour	Summary of Events and Information	Remarks and references to Appendices
SOUASTRE	26		were received for the Transport and Depot to evacuate SOUASTRE and a move in the direction of HENU was immediately commenced. A line behind which the advance of the enemy was to be checked by all troops available formed EAST of SOUASTRE.	
HENU	"		The Transport & Depot arrived in HENU at 12 noon. Rations and Baggage were sent up to the Battalion at SAILLY-AU-BOIS.	
SAILLY AU-BOIS	27		Stand-to was from 4.45 a.m. until daylight. The day passed without incident. The Battalion again completed 500A. etc. and remained ready to move into action at a moment's notice.	
	28		In accordance with Brigade Order No.116 and Battn Order No.4 the Battalion moved into billets at FAMECHON, which were reached by 6 p.m. The Brigade was addressed en route by the Divisional Commander who praised the Divisions actions during the past week. The Transport and Depot rejoined the Battalion at FAMECHON. 77 O.R. reinforcements arrived.	App. J227 App. J228

WAR DIARY
or
INTELLIGENCE SUMMARY.
(Erase heading not required.)

Army Form C. 2118.

Place	Date	Hour	Summary of Events and Information	Remarks and references to Appendices
FAMECHON (ONS 11)	1918 March 29	1.15 a.m.	At 1.15 a.m. Brigade Orders NO.147 was received and the Batt. immediately fell in to march to CANDAS and moved off at 2.10 a.m. the march proved very trying and difficult but the station was reached without casualties at 8.50 a.m. and breakfasts served. The Battalion then entrained and from Station at 9.45 a.m. CANDAS (Map. HAZEBROUCK 5A) was reached at 8.10 p.m. the Battalion detrained and personnel travelled by motor lorry to RAMILLIES CAMP (N.27.b.0.5. sheet 28 SW) which was reached at 1.35 a.m. the transport moved by road from CANDAS to DAYLIGHT CORNER and established lines at N.33.a.9.1 (sheet 28 S.W) The day was spent in cat cleaning up and baths.	App. 5230
RAMILLIES Camp.	30			
"	31		Companies reorganised and spent the day in inspections etc.	

E. Willa Lieut. Colonel
Comdg. Oxfordshire Regt.

SECRET   56th. Infantry Brigade No.B.M.891.

APP. 7200

All Battalions.
56th. T.M.Bty.
59th. Fld. Amb.   )
No.2 Coy.19th. Divl.Train.) For information

Reference 1/20,000 Sheet - MOEUVRES.

1.   The relief of 17th. Division by 19th. Division is temporarily postponed.

2.   Arrangements made for the reconnaissance of the sector to-morrow will stand.

3.   Battalions will take over in the line when the relief takes place as under:-

      <u>Right</u> 1/4th. Shrops.L.I. relieving 10th. Sherwood Foresters.
            Bn. H.Q. K.15.d.9.5.
      <u>Left</u> 9/Ches.R. relieving 7th. Border Regt. (This subsector is at
            present occupied by 7th. Lincoln Regt.)
            Bn.H.Q. K.15.d.9.5.
      <u>Support</u> 8/N.Staffs.R. relieving 7th. Lincoln Regt. (7th. Border
            Regt. are at present in support)
            Bn. H.Q. K.21.a.7.5.
      T.M's. Battery H.Q. K.21.a.7.4.

4.   Officers will proceed by Bus in accordance with S.C. 498/Q leaving BOUZINCOURT at 8 a.m. to-morrow. Each Battalion will include its Transport Officer amongst the reconnoitring party.

5.   Guides will be at the Wooden bridge on the CANAL DU NORD at J. 35 d. 9.9. at 10 a.m. to meet the busses.

6.   H.Q. 51st. Infantry Brigade is at J. 36.b.85.45. just N. of FAUGH-A-BALLAGH Bridge.

                                                            Captain,
                                                      Brigade Major,
March 4th.1918.   56th. Infantry Brigade.
A.E.

APP J 701

Z/131.

To O.C. Company.

1. Reconnoitring parties for the new Sector composed as under will report to Brigade HQ. BOUZINCOURT, at 7.45 a.m. on the 5th instant.
The party will assemble at 'D' Coy HQ. at 7.15 a.m.

HQ ... { Capt. F. H. PALMER and Intelligence Officer (Capt. BENETT-DAMPIER)
1 N.C.O. to be detailed by O.C. H.Q.

Each Coy ... { Company Commander or 2nd in Command
2. N.C. Os.

2. The busses are to proceed to HERMIES and remain there to bring parties back on completion of reconnaissance.

3. Two busses for the Brigade are going and the Senior Officer of the parties will be in charge and arrange the hour of return.

4. Details as to guides to meet reconnoitring parties will be notified later.

D. Greville 2nd Lieut
A/Adjt 9th Bn Cheshire Regt

3rd March 1918.

56th Infantry Brigade No. B.M. 916.

All Battalions.
56th T.M.Bty.
19th Div. Gas Officer (2 copies).

1. In order that the troops may have some idea of the noise and appearance of a projector discharge, the Corps Chemical Adviser will give a demonstration of projectors on the evening of the 6th March, under the following arrangements.

2. The demonstration will be carried out at V.12.c.5.5. (Central). The projectors being fixed from the track running N.E. from that point in a N.W. direction.

3. Battalions will arrive at the Cross Roads V.12.c.6.5. at the following times:-

    1/4th Shrops. L.I.   5.30 p.m.
    8th N.Staff. Regt.   5.35 p.m.
    9th Ches. Regt.   5.40 p.m.

and will proceed to their forming up positions as under

    1/4th Shrops. L.I.   On track running N.E. from the Cross roads - N. and well clear of the projector position.

    8th N.Staff. Regt.   On the HEDAUVILLE - BOUZINCOURT Road - Rear of Battalion to be 250 yards from the Cross Roads.

    9th Ches. Regt.   S.E. of the 8th N.Staff. Regt. on the same road, but to keep clear of the Cross Roads.

4. Men will be kept in fours, closed up as much as possible and on the side of the road.

5. The Chemical Adviser will go round to the position of Battalions and address the men in explanation of details of the demonstration, as soon as Battalions are in position.

6. Company Commanders will ensure that their men understand the meaning of projector attacks before they come to the demonstration and that their attention is especially directed to

    (a) The noise and appearance of the discharge.
    (b) The time of flight of the bomb.
    (c) The appearance of the bomb (i.e. fuze burning).
    (d) The duration in time of the flight - that period being the time in which it is necessary for them to be able to get their box respirators on, in the event of an actual projector attack.

7. The projectors will be discharged about 6.0 p.m.

8. On completion of the demonstration each Battalion will let off one S.O.S. Rifle Grenade Signal in order that troops may have an opportunity of seeing what the signal looks like by night.

9. 56th T.M.Bty. will march out to ground in rear of, and take up a position on the ground on the same track as and just S.W. of, 1/4th Shrops. L.I.

10. When the S.O.S. signal has been fired, as in para.8, units will march back to billets.

5th March 1918.
A.J.G.

Captain,
Brigade Major,
56th Infantry Brigade.

56th Infantry Brigade No. B.M.916/1.

All Battalions.
56th T.M.Bty.

In continuation of B.M.916 of yesterday, Units will parade in clean fatigue dress without arms.

6th March 1918.
A.J.G.

Captain,
for Brigade Major,
56th Infantry Brigade.

Headquarters
56th Infantry Brigade

Ref: B.M. 916.

As we have no squared map in our possession showing this area, will you please give place of gas projector demonstration & of rendezvous in references for LENS II map.

D. Lewis Capt.
for Major
Cmdg. 9 Cheshire Regt.

5/3/18.

9 Ches. R.
─────────

Where the SENLIS road joins the main ALBERT-DOULLENS Rd ¾ mile due West of BOUZINCOURT CHURCH

6-3-18.

for B.M.

APP J203

2/146

To O.C. Coy.

1. The following Officers will proceed to the forward area to carry out a special reconnaissance.

H.Q. ... { Commanding Officer
         { Intelligence Officer (Capt. Dampier)

A Coy ... { Capt. F. FULLER.
          { 2nd Lt. A. RILEY.

B Coy ... { 2nd Lt. R.S. WELCH.
          { 2nd Lt. J.W. BROOKES.

C Coy ... { Capt. A.R. WALTON (if O.C.Coy is
          { 2nd Lt. J. WILKINSON not well enough)
                                (2nd Lt. VERITY)

D Coy ... { Lieut. J.A. BAIRD.
          { 2nd Lt. W.N. STUBBS.

2. These Officers will proceed by two busses leaving Brigade H.Q. at 8.30 a.m. The busses will proceed to the road junction S. of HERMIES, J.35.a.6.8 where parties will debus. Transport Officer will arrange for the C.O's horse and all Coy horses to be at the respective messes at 8.a.m. The Adjutant's horse will be at "C" Coy H.Q. for Captain Dampier. The Mess Cart will be at "D" Coy H.Q. where Officers not riding will assemble at 7.45 a.m and be conveyed to Brigade H.Q. by the Mess Cart. Transport Officer will arrange for 4 grooms to be at Brigade H.Q. by 8.15.a.m in order to bring back the horses.

3. Busses will be under the orders of the Senior Officer. They will wait and bring the party back on completion of the reconnaissance.

4. Officers of these parties will meet the Brigade Commander at the junction of the Road and Railway J.29.d.05.90 at 11.30 a.m.

5. Sandwiches should be taken, also maps 1/20,000 MOEUVRES and 1/40,000 Sheet 57c. and field glasses & prismatic compasses. Steel Helmets and box Respirators will be carried.

6. Parties may expect to get back to billets about 6.0 p.m.

D. Presillie Capt.
A/Adjt 9th Bn Cheshire Rgt

URGENT.   56th Infantry Brigade NO. B.M. 891/1.

All Battalions.
56th T.M.Bty.

     Reference B.M. 891 of this evening, please ensure that your reconnoitring parties tomorrow pay especial attention ~~attention~~ to reconnoitring the second system and the lines of approach thereto.

4th March 1918.
A.J.G.

Captain,
Brigade Major,
56th Infantry Brigade.

Z/160.

To O.C. Coy.,

APP J204

An advance party consisting of 2/Lt C.R.PAINTER and 1 N.C.O. per Coy,H.Q. and Transport (6 in all) will report at Battalion H.Q. at 12 noon today - Dress full marching order ; blankets and rations to be taken.

Each N.C.O. is to have the billeting requirements of his Company. 2/Lt Painter will report to the Adjutant at 12 noon.

Transport Officer will detail transport to carry equipment etc. of above to Brigade H.Q. - report to Battalion H.Q. at above time.

J. Smith
Capt,
A/Adjt 8th Bn The Cheshire Regt.

6:7:18.

SECRET   COPY No. 23

56th. Infantry Brigade Order No.113

Reference 1/100,000
Sheet 11 (LENS)   6.3.18.

1. The 56th. Inf. Bde. Group will move by train on 7th. inst. to the BEAULENCOURT Area taking over the camps now occupied by 57th. Inf. Bde.

2. Units will move to the Entraining station (AVELUY) passing the respective Starting Points as under:-

	Starting Point	Time at which Head of Unit passes S.P.
1/4th. Shrops L.I. (less transport)	BOUZINCOURT Church	7-20 a.m.
9/Ches.R. (less transport)	Road junction ½ mile W. of BOUZINCOURT on BOUZINCOURT - SENLIS Road	7-15 a.m.
8/N.Staffs.R. (less transport)	- do -	7-25 a.m.
Transport. 1/4th Shrops. L.I.	BOUZINCOURT Church.	7-40 a.m.
Transport. 9th Ches. Regt.	- do -	7-45 a.m.
Transport. 8th N.Staff. Regt.	- do -	9-15 a.m.
Transport. Bde. H.Q.	- do -	9-20 a.m.
Transport. 59th Fd. Amb.	Billets.	9-40 a.m.
Bde. H.Q. (Personnel)	BOUZINCOURT Church.	10-30 a.m.
56th T.M.Bty.	- do -	10-33 a.m.
59th Fd. Amb. (less Transport)	Billets.	11-0 a.m.

No.2 Coy. 19th Div. Train will proceed by road under their own arrangements.

3. The usual 10 minutes halt at 10 minutes to each clock hour will be observed.

4. Details as to entrainment and administrative arrangements have already been issued by the Staff Captain.

5. On arrival at the detraining Station (BAPAUME) units will proceed direct by route march to their camps in accordance with the next paragraph.

6. Units will be accommodated in the BEAULENCOURT area as under:-

> 9th Ches. Regt.   Take over from 8th Glouc. Regt.
> Camp at N.24.b.3.0.
> 1/4th Shrops. L.I. Take over from 10th Worc. Regt.
> Camp at N.18.a.2.0.
> 8th N.Staff. Regt. Take over from 10th R.War. Regt.
> Camp at N.18.c.6.4.
> 56th T.M.Bty.   Taking over from 57th T.M.Bty.
> N.24.a.8.7.
> 59th Fd. Ambulance. To be notified later.
>
> No.2 Coy. Div. Train. - BARASTRE.

7. Bde. H.Q. will close at BOUZINCOURT at 8.30 a.m. on 7th inst. and reopen at BEAULENCOURT (N.24.a.8.7.) at 3 p.m. on the same day.

8. ACKNOWLEDGE.

Issued at 7.0 a.m.

Bde. H.Q.
A.J.G.

                              Captain,
                          Brigade Major,
                     56th Infantry Brigade.

Copies to:-

1. 19th Div. "G".
2. 19th Div. "Q".
3. 57th Inf. Bde.
4. 58th Inf. Bde.
5. 9th Ches. R.
6. 1/4th Shrops. L.I.
7. 8th N.Staff. R.
8. 56th T.M.Bty.
9. 59th Fd. Ambulance.
10. No.2 Coy. 19th Div. Train.
11. A.D.M.S. 19th Div.
12. A.P.M. 19th Div.
13. 19th Div. Train.
14. R.T.O. AVELUY.
15. Area Commandant, BEAULENCOURT.
16. G.O.C.
17. Staff Captain.
18. War Diary.
19. File.

SECRET.
                     56th Infantry Brigade
                  ADMINISTRATIVE INSTRUCTIONS No. 8.
                 (Issued with reference to Brigade Order No.113)

   Ref.Map.
     1/100,000 LENS.

1. MOVE.   The 56th Brigade Group will move by rail from AVELUY
                 to BAPAUME in accordance with the attached entraining
                 table and instructions.
                     No.2 Coy. 19th Div. Train and Baggage and Supply Section
                 will proceed by road under orders of O.C. No.2 Coy. 19th
                 Div. Train.
                     Baggage wagons of units will rendezvous in BOUZINCOURT
                 at Refilling Point at 8.0 a.m. 7th instant.
                     M.T. and 6 G.S. wagons of 59th Field Ambulance will
                 proceed by road under orders of the Officer Commanding.

2. SUPPLY   Railhead from the 7th instant inclusive will be
   ARRANGEMENTS. ROCQUIGNY.
                     Refilling on the 7th instant will take place at
                 BEAULENCOURT at 4.30 p.m.
                     Units will ensure that guides attend at Refilling.
                     The Supply Section will travel unloaded on the 7th
                 instant, the supply lorries conveying supplies and
                 dumping at the New Refilling Point on arrival.

3. EXTRA
   TRANSPORT.   Allotment of extra transport is shown on the attached
                 lorry table.

4. RETURN OF   All billet stores will be handed over by units before
   BILLET STORES.they leave, to the local billet wardens.
                     Certificates that billets have been left in a satis-
                 factory condition will be obtained from the Area
                 Commandant or his representative, and forwarded to this
                 office.

5. BATHS.   The Baths at SENLIS will close at 6.0 p.m. 6th inst.
                 and personnel in charge will return to their units.

6. BILLETING   Advance Billeting parties consisting of one officer
   PARTIES.   and 6 other ranks per battalion and one officer and 5 other
                 ranks per other unit will report at Bde. H.Q. at 1.0 p.m.
                 tomorrow bringing one day's rations and blankets, and will
                 proceed to the new area by motor lorry.

7. LOCATIONS.   A location table showing locations in the BEAULENCOURT
                 area is attached.

8.   ACKNOWLEDGE.

                 Issued at 7 a.m.

                                                  Captain,
                                                  Staff Captain,
                                          56th. Infantry Brigade.

March 6th, 1918.

Copies to:-

1. 9th Ches. Regt.
2. 1/4th Shrops. L.I.
3. 8th N. Staff. Regt.
4. 56th T.M.Bty.
5. 59th Fd. Ambulance.
6. No.2 Coy. Div. Train.
7. 19th Div. "G".
8. 19th Div. "Q".
9. A.D.M.S.
10. A.P.M.
11. H.Q. 19th Div. Train.
12. Area Commandant, BOUZINCOURT.
13. Traffic, ALBERT.
14. R.T.O. AVELUY.
15. R.T.O. ~~BUENTCOURT~~. Bapaume
16. G.O.C.
17. Brigade Major.
18. Signals.
19. War Diary.
20. File.

TRAIN TABLE.

1. **PERSONNEL TRAIN** (50 Covered trucks)

    AVELUY   dep. 9-0 a.m.
    BAPAUME   arr. 11-0 a.m.

    Troops to proceed

    9/Ches.R.   (less 1st. line Transport & 3 Off. 150 O.Rs)
    1/4th. Shrop.L.("   "   "   "   "   " "   "   ")
    8/N.Staffs.R. ("   "   "   "   "   " "   "   ")
    56th. T.M.Bty. complete.

2. **No. 1 OMNIBUS TRAIN**, (30 Covered trucks, 17 flats)

    AVELUY   dep. 10 a.m.
    BAPAUME   arr. 12 noon

    Troops to proceed

    3 Off. 150 O.Rs. 9/Ches. R. and 1st Line Transport.
    3 Off. 150 O.Rs. 1/4th. Shrops.LI. and 1st. Line Transport.

3. **No. 2 OMNIBUS TRAIN.** (30 covered trucks, 17 flats)

    AVELUY   dep. 12 noon
    BAPAUME   arr. 2 p.m.

    Troops to proceed

    3 Officers & 150 O.Rs. 8/N.Staffs.R. and 1st Line Transport.
    59th. Fld. Amb. (less M.T., Horse Ambulances and six G.S. wagons.
    Brigade Headquarters complete.

NOTE.
    The 3 Officers and 150 O.Rs. of battalions proceeding on the Omnibus Train includes 1st. Line Transport.personnel.

LORRY TABLE

Lorries are allotted to units as under:-

    Each Battalion   3
    56th. T.M.Bty.   2
    59th. Field Amb.   1.

Guides for these lorries will report at Brigade Headquarters at 7.30 A.M. 7th. inst.

INSTRUCTIONS WITH REFERENCE TO THE MOVE BY RAIL.
----

1. Personnel will arrive one hour, and transport two hours, before the train is scheduled to leave the entraining station.
    Transport Officers will report to the R.T.O. at the Entraining Station half an hour before the arrival of the Transport of ~~their~~ unit.

2. Each unit will provide a party of one Officer and 50 O.R. for entraining and detraining their own transport. This party will be found from personnel proceeding on the omnibus train.

3. Each Battalion will detail one Entraining Officer to report to the R.T.O's Office AVELUY one hour before the departure of the personnel train.
    O.C. 8th M. Staff. Regt. will detail one Detraining Officer to report at the R.T.O's office FREMICOURT on the arrival of the first train.

4. Battalion entraining officers will bring entraining states with them.
    Other units will arrange to send states to the R.T.O. AVELUY half an hour before they arrive at the station.

LOCATION TABLE.
BEAULENCOURT AREA

```
9/Ches.R.            take over from   8/Glouc.R.       at N.24.b.3.0.
1/4th.Shrop.L.I.       "    "    "    10/Worc. R.      at N.18.a.2.0.
8/N.Staff.R.           "    "    "    10/R.War.R.      at N.18.c.6.4.
56th. T.M.Bty.         "    "    "    57th.T.M.Bty.    at N.24.a.8.7.
59th. Fld. Amb.      ------------     BEAULENCOURT Area.✱
No." Coy. 19th. Div.Train.....        BARASTRE Area.✱
```

✱ Exact location to be notified later.

9th (5) Bn. Cheshire Regt.   6-3-18.
Orders No 3

Reference Map. LENS 11.
 Sheet 57c.

 Reveille 5.0 a.m.
 Breakfast 5.30 a.m.
 Dinners in Camp. at 11.0 p.m.
 Dry ration to be carried on the man.

1. The 56th Inf. Brigade Group will move by train tomorrow the 7th inst to the BEAULENCOURT Area.

2. Entraining Station :- AVELUY.
 Detraining " BAPAUME.

3. The Battalion will parade in full marching order in column of route, ready to move off at 6.55 a.m. In the order:-
 Band. B. C. D. A. HQ.
 head of the column being at junction of track and road at 6.H.O.3. - and march to AVELUY, where it is due to arrive at 8 a.m.
 On arrival at BAPAUME (11.a.m) the Battn. will again form up in column of route as above and march to camp at N.24. b.3.0.

4. Normal halts will be observed, i.e. halt at 10 minutes to every clock hour.

5. Transport will move under orders to be issued separately to Transport Officer.

6. O.C. "D" Coy will detail a party of 1 Officer and 70 O.R. to travel with the Transport. This party will march in front of the Transport and will travel on No1 Omnibus Train with the Transport. They will assist in entraining and detraining the transport. Time of parade will be arranged between O C "D" Coy and the Transport Officer.

7. All Lewis Guns and L.G. Equipment as already detailed in Bn. Orders will be loaded up today also all other stores that travel on the Transport or limbers.

8. Blankets tightly rolled and clearly labelled in bundles of 10, Officers kits etc, are to be stacked at Company HQ. by 6.15 a.m. The Quartermaster will arrange to collect these as soon as the lorries arrive. Each Company will leave a guard of two men (bad marchers) over the above who will remain behind and travel with the lorries.

-2-

9. All tables and forms in Coys' possession that are billet stores are to be handed over to the billet warden by 6.15 a.m tomorrow, billets must be left scrupulously clean and all rubbish burnt or buried. This must be done by 6.15 a.m in order to enable the Area Commandant to inspect billets and give a certificate of cleanliness

10. Brigade HQ. will close at BOUZINCOURT at 8.30 a.m on 7th inst and reopen at BEAULENCOURT (N.24.a.8.7) at 3. p.m the same day.

Copy No 1 C.O
         2 2i/c
         3 Adjt
         4 File
         5 A Coy
         6 B
         7 C
         8 D
         9 HQ
        10 TO
        11 QM
        12 w/o

D. Greville Capt.
Adjutant 9th Bn Cheshire Regt

56th Infantry Brigade No. B.M. 918.

SECRET and URGENT.

APP J 207   C9

All Battalions.
56th T.M.Bty.
---

1. The 19th Division is at present the Left Reserve Division of the V Corps.

2. The most probable action of the Left Reserve Division, in the event of hostile attack, is as follows:-

   (a) To occupy any portion of the Battle Zone ordered, especial attention being paid to the occupation of the Second System from the TRESCAULT - FLESQUIERES Road in Q.4.b. (inclusive) to the Corps Northern Boundary in J.24.a.

   (b) To counter-attack towards HAVRINCOURT.

   (c) To counter-attack towards HERMIES.

   (d) To assist the IV Corps (on the left of the V Corps) by counter-attack to regain DEMICOURT, DOIGNIES, or LOUVERVAL.

   (e) To relieve troops holding the line.

3. The Infantry Brigades have been ordered by the Division to carry out daily reconnaissances of portions of this area, until satisfied that troops would be able to assemble rapidly by day or night for the following purposes:-

   (a) To occupy the 2nd and 3rd Systems.

   (b) To counter-attack
       From the Second System towards HAVRINCOURT or DEMICOURT.

       From the Third System towards HERMIES, DOIGNIES or LOUVERVAL.

4. A map is issued herewith shewing the Second and Third Systems within the area, bounded on the South by a line joining RUYAULCOURT and TRESCAULT, and on the North by a line joining LE BUCQUIERE and LOUVERVAL. It is of great importance that officers should make themselves fully acquainted with this area and the Second and Third Systems and the approaches thereto.
   For the purpose of reconnaissance the map has been divided by pencil lines into three areas (A, B, & C.), each of which roughly corresponds to the frontage which might be held by one Brigade for defensive purposes.*

5. In order not to interfere with training, Reconnaissances in accordance with paras. 3 and 4 will be carried out each afternoon when the Brigade has moved up to the Forward Area on the 7th instant. A reconnaissance lasting the whole day will be carried out tomorrow, 6th instant, in accordance with details already issued

*(NOTE - Owing to the sheet South of the MOEUVRES sheet not being available the map only shews that portion of area A. North of the Southern edge of the map.)

6.   Each such reconnaissance will cover at least one area, i.e. A, B, or C. The C.O. or 2nd in Command of the Battalion and the Os.C., or 2nd in Command, of each Company, together with not less than one other officer and two N.C.Os. per Company should carry out these reconnaissances.

7.   Special attention is to be paid as to the selection of the best routes by which Companies can be brought forward by day to man the 2nd and 3rd Systems. BERTINCOURT itself should not be regarded as a suitable line of approach for troops moving up for this purpose, as it would certainly be congested with traffic and would probably be shelled during a heavy attack.

8.   Details as to the Transport arrangements and area which is to be reconnoitred each day will be issued on the preceding evening after arrival in the New Area.

9.   Care should be taken that reconnoitring parties do not "bunch" when under direct observation, in order that they may not draw hostile shell fire.

5th March 1918.
A.J.G.

Captain,
Brigade Major,
56th Infantry Brigade.

SECRET

56th Infantry Brigade No. B.M.1057.

6 copies

All Battns.
56th T.M.Bty.
19th Divn."G.")
57th Inf. Bde.) for information.

Ref. 1/40,000 sheet MOEUVRES.

1. Portions of the Second and Third Systems have been indicated by 19th Divn. as those which the Brigade may be required to hold defensively.
   These are as follows:-
   Second System.
      Sector E. - J.10.d.25.20 to J.3.b.40.35.
   Third System.
      Sector J. - J.28.a.75.35 to J.15.d.0.53.
      Sector K. - J.15.d.0.3. to J.7.b.4.2.

2. The following paragraphs contain the allotments of frontages and approximate dispositions which will be taken up by Battalions in the event of the Brigade being ordered to occupy any of these.
   Each Sector will be held with two Battalions in the Line and one in reserve.

3. Sector E. (Second System).
   Right Battalion (1/4 Shrops. L.I.) - J.10.d.25.20 to J.10.a.85.90
   Three Companies in the Line. One Company in Support as follows
   Company Headquarters and two Platoons - about J.15.d.8.8.(old Gun positions).- Two Platoons about J.9.c.(old Gun positions.)
   Battalion H.Q. J.14.b.75.05.
   Left Battalion. - (8th.Staffs. R.) J.10.a.85.90 to J.3.b.40.35.
   Three Companies in the Line. One Company in Support -LOUVERVAL RESERVE and dugout about J.3.c.95.55.
   Battalion H.Q. J.14.b.1.0.
   Reserve Battalion (9th Ches.R.)
   One Company in Third System about J.14.d.8.5.
   One Company in Third System about J.8.c.1.5.
   Battalion H.Q. and two Companies - BEAUMETZ.

4. Sector J. (Third System).
   Right Battalion (9th Ches. R.) - J.28.a.75.35 to J.21.b.7.1.
   Three Companies in the Line. One Company in Support - about J.26.b.30.0.5.
   Battalion H.Q. J.20.c.6.6.
   Left Battalion. (1/4th Shrops L.I. - J.21.b.7.1. to J.15.d.0.3.
   Three Companies in the Line , One Company in Support about J.20.c.6.8.
   Battalion H.Q. J.20.c.6.6.
   Reserve Battalion. (8th N.Staffs.R.) - VELU.
      Note. There is ample dugout accommodation in the sunken road in J.20.c.

5. Sector K. (Third System).
   Right Battalion. (9th Ches.R.) - J.15.d.0.3. to J.14.b.0.7. (point where line of telegraph post crosses Third System).
   Three Companies in the Line, one Company in Support about J.19.b.5.3.
   Battalion H.Q. J.19.b.5.5. (catacombs).
   Left Battalion. (8th N.Staffs. R.). J.14.b.0.7. to J.7.b.4.2.
   Three Companies in the Line, one Company in Support about J.13.c.
   Battalion H.Q. J.19.b.5.5. (catacombs).
   Reserve Battalion. (1/4 Shrops. L.I.) - LEBUCQUIERE.

6. Companies in the Line will be invariably disposed in depth. In the case of Sectors J and K full use will be made of the road which runs from 100 to 400 yards in rear of the Third System across the whole of both sectors, and is in many places sunken and already containing shelters or dugouts.

Where no cover exists to allow of disposition in depth, reserve Platoons of Companies will be ordered to dig in.

7. "Coys ~~with~~ in the line will be ~~A B C~~ ~~D~~ A right B Centre C left"

14th March, 1918.
G.R.O.

C. O'Connell
Captain,
Brigade Major,
50th Infantry Brigade.

56th Infantry Brigade No. B.M. 1113.

All Battalions.
Bds. Signal Section.
----

1. In continuation of my B.M. 1086/1 of today, herewith is forwarded copy of tactical exercise with Tanks to be carried out tomorrow morning, also copy of map referred to.

2. The exercise will be carried out by 9th Ches. Regt.

3. The enemy, one complete company not less than 100 strong, will be represented under the arrangements of O.C. 1/4th Shrops. L.I. who will detail the Company Commander to post and direct their operations. Positions will be selected in all strips of trench between the objectives as well as in the objectives themselves.
   O.C. 1/4th Shrops. L.I. will arrange for the supply of blank, each man should be provided with 5 rounds.
   Men should also be provided with tins on which they will beat to represent the fire of M.Gs.

4. The barrage will be represented by a party detailed by 8th N.Staff. Regt. Details as to the time and place at which the barrage party is to report, will be notified later. The party will be under an Officer who will co-operate with the Officer detailed by the G.R.A. to organise the barrage.

5. The advance by 9th Ches. Regt. will be carried out on a three company frontage, each company on a platoon frontage (i.e. with two half platoons in the first wave).

6. 8th N.Staff. Regt. will detail two senior officers not below the rank of Coy. Commander to act as umpires. These officers will wear white arm-bands and will meet the Brigade Major in front of the jumping off line at 9.45 a.m.

7. Men not taking part in the operations will be marched out to and take up a position on the high ground just W. of BARASTRE from which they can witness the advance.

8. Troops will be in position by the following hours:-

   9th Ches. Regt. 9.45 a.m. - drawn up behind the jumping off line ready to advance.

   1/4th Shrops. L.I. - enemy - 9.30 a.m.

   Spectators - 9.55 a.m.

   8th N.Staff. Regt. - barrage party - To be notified later.

   Spectators - 9.55 a.m.

9. A watch will be sent round Battalions at 9.0 p.m. tonight in order that watches may be synchronised.
   Another watch will be sent round at 7.30 a.m. tomorrow morning in order to further check the synchronisation.

10. The Brigade Advanced report centre will be at GAIKA Copse at the beginning of the operations. O.C. Bde. Signal Section will arrange to establish an Advanced report centre about the Cross Road C.17.b.8.8. as soon as possible after the capture of the first objective.

11. Smoke screens on the objectives are being carried out under Divisional arrangements.

19th March 1918.
A.J.G.

Captain,
Brigade Major,
56th Infantry Brigade.

SECRET.
19th Division
G.T.405.

TACTICAL EXERCISE WITH TANKS. No. 3.

GENERAL IDEA.

The Trench lines A-B, C-D, E-F on the attached map represent the British 1st, 2nd and 3rd Systems of Defence, respectively, facing Westwards.

At dawn on 20th March the Germans attacked and captured the British 1st and 2nd Systems.

At Zero — 6 hours the British and German front lines were definitely located by aeroplanes as running along the Blue and Red Lines, respectively, shown on the attached map.

SPECIAL IDEA.

1. At Zero — 4 hours the 56th Inf. Bde. which has been concentrated in VELU WOOD receives orders to counter-attack and retake the British 1st System. 4 Sections of No. 10 Battn. of Tanks will lead the attack. Other troops are attacking on either flank.

2. The Jumping-off Line, Objectives and Boundaries of the Left Battn. of 56th Inf. Bde. and 2 Sections of Tanks are shown on the attached map.

   The Right Battn. and the other 2 Sections of Tanks are, for the purposes of the Scheme, imaginary.

3. The rates of advance of the Infantry will be as follows :-

   From Jumping-off line to 1st Objective 100 yards in 2 mins.
   From 1st Objective to 2nd Objective 100 yards in 3 mins.
   Pause of 5 mins. on 2nd Objective.
   From 2nd Objective to 3rd Objective 100 yards in 3 mins.
   Pause of 5 mins. on 3rd Objective.
   From 3rd Objective to Final Objective 100 yards in 3 mins.

4. The Field Artillery at Zero will place a standing barrage on the 1st Objective and at O plus 14 will lift on to the 2nd Objective.

   The subsequent lifts off the various Objectives will be made at the times shown on the attached map, care being taken, however, to deal with any isolated bits of trench, or gun-pits situated between the various Objectives.

   The time at which the Artillery lifts off each Objective is based on the supposition that the tanks will be then 80 yards from the Objective, and the Infantry about 120 yards behind the tanks.

5. Arrangements will be made to place a smoke screen on the 2nd Objective from O plus 10 to O plus 30, on the 3rd Objective from O plus 35 to O plus 70, and on the Final Objective from O plus 70 to O plus 95.

6. D.M.G.C. will arrange for a M.G. barrage to cover the advance.

7. Adv. Bde. Report Centre will be at GAIKA COPSE (O.6.b.)

8. Zero hour will be 10 a.m.

9. Watches will be synchronised by O.C. 19th Divl. Signals at 7 a.m.

NOTES.

(a) The enemy will be represented by small parties of men and Lewis Guns placed in trenches, shell holes, gun-pits etc. These men will wear caps, be provided with blank ammunition, and should number at least 100. A senior officer will place the enemy in position and 2 senior officers will be detailed by the Bde. to act as Umpires.

(b) All available Infantry of the Bde. carrying out the exercise and who are not taking part, will be placed at convenient points from which they can watch the exercise.

(c) The Infantry will commence the advance in small columns moving behind the Tanks. These columns will extend when required to fire and will at once close up to the Tanks when the latter reach an objective or defended bit of trench. The Advance will be carried out as in open warfare, i.e. by taking advantage of all cover, by moving in rushes over exposed ground, and by using covering fire.

(d) The Barrage will be represented by men waving flags. The Tanks should not approach nearer than 80 yards to the Barrage.

56th Inf. Bde. will provide 40 men with flags to represent the Barrage which will be worked by an officer to be detailed by C.R.A. who will inform 56th Inf. Bde. of the time and place at which these men should report.

SECRET. Copy No. 7.

56th Infantry Brigade Order No.114.

Ref. 1/40,000 Sheet 57c.   20-3-1918.

1. The 56th Inf.Bde. will relieve 52nd Inf.Bde. in the Right Brigade Sector of the CANAL Sector of the Corps Front on the night 23/24th March.
   On completion of the relief 188th Inf.Bde. will be on the right and 58th Inf. Bde. on the left of the Brigade Front.

2. Reliefs will be carried out in accordance with the attached table. Any details not laid down herein will be arranged between C.Os.concerned.

3. The following advance parties from Units will proceed on 22nd March spending the night 22nd/23rd March in the line.
   1/4th Shrops. L.I. and 9th Ches. Regt.
     1 Officer 1 N.C.O. and 2 Runners per Company.
     Battalion Intelligence Officer and 2 Battalion Runners.
   8th N. Staffs. Regt.
     1 Officer and 4 Runners to join the forward Companies.
   56th T.M.Bty.
     1 Officer and 1 N.C.O.
   These parties will report at Brigade H.Q.-BEAULENCOURT at 2. 0. p.m. They will be taken by lorry to the Spoil Heap in J.34.d, whence they will proceed direct to the H.Qrs. of the respective Units which they are relieving.

4. Units will be carried to the Forward Area on 23rd March by train - entraining at ROCQUIGNY and detraining in Q.2.d. in accordance with detailed orders which are being issued by the Staff Captain.

5. Transport Lines move to VELU Wood. These will be allotted by the Staff Captain.

6. All Trench stores, secret maps and Defence Schemes will be taken over on relief. Lists showing the amount taken over will be forwarded to Bde. H.Q. by 6 p.m. 24th March. Units will hand over to Units of 52nd Inf. Bde. all tactical schemes and details of training in the present area.

7. Reports to Bde. H.Q. on completion of the relief by wiring the initials of the Adjutant.

8. Brigade H.Q. will close at BEAULENCOURT at 5.30 p.m. on 23rd March and reopen at J.36.b.5.4. at the same hour.

9. ACKNOWLEDGE.

                                          Captain,
                                          Brigade Major.
                                          56th Infantry Brigade.

Issued at 8.0.p.m.
Copies to :-
1. 19th Division "G".   No. 9. 8th N.Staffs.R.   No. 17. H.Q.19th Div.Tn.
2. 19th Division "Q".   10. 56th T.M.Bty.   18. No.2 Coy.Train.
3. 52nd Inf. Bde.   11. Signals.   19. G.O.C.
4. 57th Inf. Bde.   12. C.R.A.   20. Staff Captain.
5. 58th Inf. Bde.   13. C.R.E.   21. Bde. T.O.
6. 188th Inf. Bde.   14. D.M.G.C.   22. T.O.7/R.Lanc.R.
7. 9th Ches. R.   15. A.D.M.S.   23. War Diary.
8. 1/4th Shrops. L.I.   16. A.P.M.   24. File.

Table of Reliefs. — Appendix to 56th Inf. Bde. Order No.114.

Unit.	From.	Handing over to.	To.	Taking over from.	Remarks.
9th Ches.R.	BEAULENCOURT G.Camp.	10th Lanc.Fus.	Left Subsector. (Bn.H.Q.,K.15.d.9.5.)	10th Lancs.Fus.	Not to pass the line of HAVRINCOURT-HERMIES Road before 7.30 p.m.
1/4th Shrops.L.I.	Do. A. Camp.	12th Lanch. Regt.	Right subsector (bn.H.Q. K.15d.9.3.)	12th Lanch. Regt.	- Do. - Before 8.0.p.m.
8th N. Staffs.	Do. F.Camp.	9th W.Rid. R.	Support subsector. (Bn.H.Q.,K.21a.7.5.	9th W.Rid.R.	-
56th T.M.Bty.	Do. G. Camp.	52nd T.M.Bty.	Line. (Battery H.Q., K.21.a. 7.5.)	52nd T.M.Bty.	To relieve by daylight.

NOTES.

1. Units of 52nd Infantry Bde. are providing guides at the rate of 1 per platoon and 1 for Bn. and each Company H.Q. - Rendezvous will be arranged direct by Os.C. concerned.

2. All movement will be by platoons at 100 yds. distance.

3. Disposition reports will be forwarded to Bde. H.Q. by 9.30 a.m. 24th inst.

Bde. H.Q.,
20-3-1918.
C.R.C.

"A" Form
MESSAGES AND SIGNALS.

Army Form C. 2121

TO: All Battalions

M.830 20/3/18   AAA

Herewith Sketch Map
Showing Dispositions
in 52nd Infy Brigade
Area

From: 56th Inf Bde

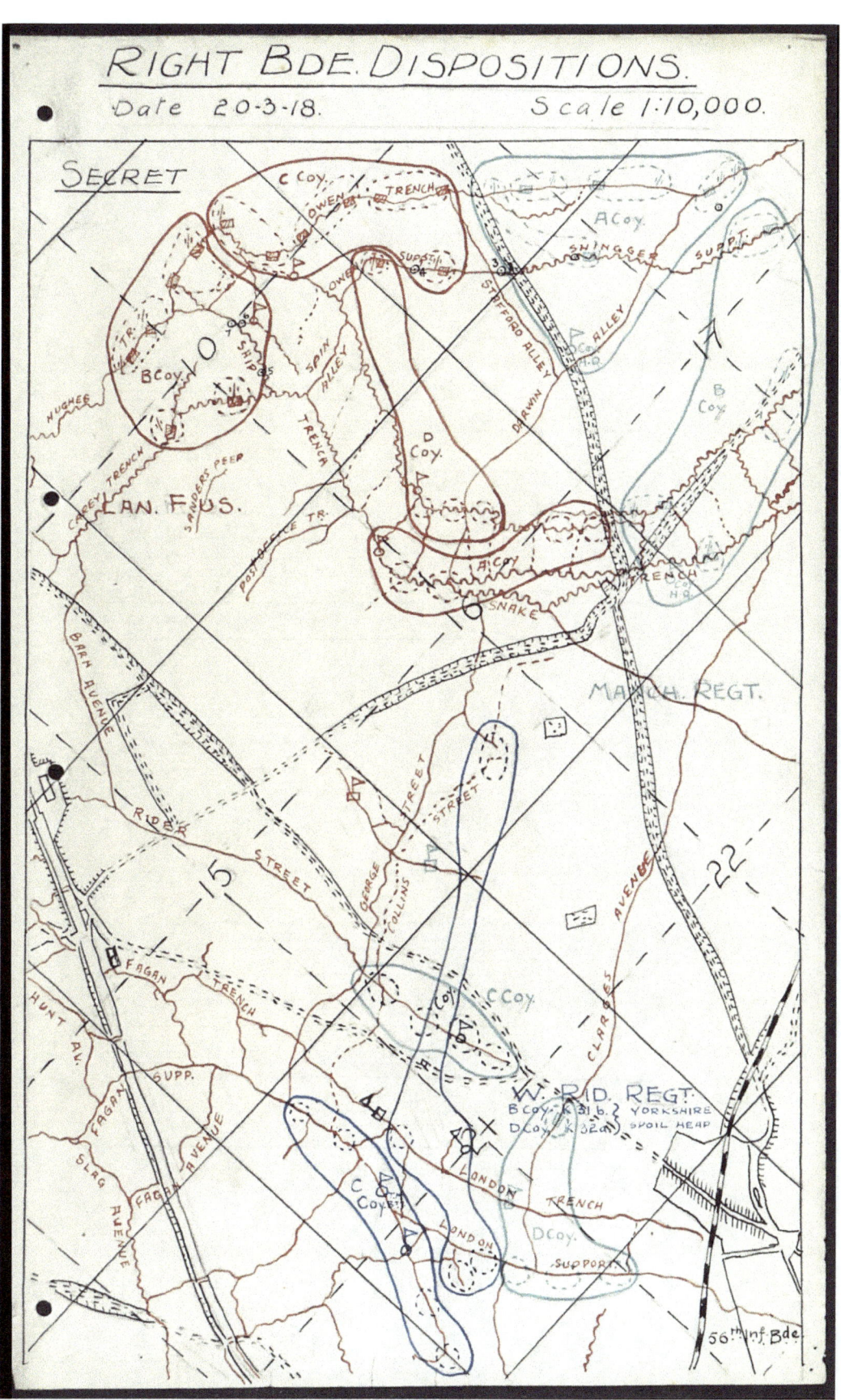

APP J213

"C" Form
MESSAGES AND SIGNALS.
Army Form C. 2123.

| Prefix | Code | Words | Received From | Sent, or sent out At | Office Stamp |

Handed in at .... Office ...... m. Received ...... m.

TO All Units

*Sender's Number	Day of Month	In reply to Number	AAA
GA549	21		

STAND BY and
acknowledge

5.35 am

FROM / PLACE & TIME   56 Bde

Appendix J 213 (a)

Names of Officers who went into action with the battalion on Thursday 21st March 1918

Headquarters
Cmdg. Major G.K. Fulton
Adjutant Capt. D. Greville
Intelligence
 Officer Lieut. R.C.W. Bewett-Dampier
Signalling
 Officer " E. Simcock
Medical Officer
 (attached) Major A. Walker (R.A.M.C. (T))

Companies

A Capt. F.H. Palmer (Cmdg)   C 2/Lt G.H. Verity (Cmdg)
   Lieut J.R. Mallalieu   " V.E. Hamahries
   2/Lt W.M. Owen   " J.W.W. Kinson
      W. Carruthers

B 2/Lt Ray. C. (Cmdg)   D Capt. A.D. Milner (Cmdg)
    " R.S. Walsh   Lieut C.H. Jones
    " J.W. Brookes   2/Lt W.M. Stubbs

                                        Adjutant.

APP J 21

"A" Form — Army Form C. 2121
MESSAGES AND SIGNALS. No. of Message

TO: All Battalions
   36 TM Bty

Sender's Number: BM 632   Day of Month: 21   AAA

Move to camps. ZERO hour 12 (noon)

From: 36th Inf Bde

Capt.

A 22/165.

"All coys, T.O. & QM.

Move to camps. Zero hour
Broon — parade on football
ground Broon.

11.40 a.m.   D Grenfell Capt.
21/3/18   Adjt.

A
B
C
D   — 11.50.
HQ
T.O.   T.O
QM

"A" Form Army Form C. 2121
MESSAGES AND SIGNALS. No. of Message..........

Prefix......Code......m.	Words	Charge	This message is on a/c of	Recd. at......m.
Office of Origin and Service Instructions.	Sent		APP J 215	Date..........
	At......m.		Service.	From..........
	To..........			
	By..........	(Signature of "Franking Officer.")	By..........

TO All Units

| Sender's Number. | Day of Month. | In reply to Number. | AAA |
| BM.466/S | 21. 3. 18 | | |

9th Division is to counterattack
JOIGNIES 56th Inf Bde will
be in reserve; detailed orders
follow

From: 56th Inf Bde
Place:
Time:

S E C R E T.

App J216

56th INFANTRY BRIGADE ORDER No.115.

Reference.
1/20,000 Sheet MOEUVRES.   21. 3. 1918.

1. The enemy hold LOUVERVAL and DOIGNIES West of the DOIGNIES - BOURSIES Road. 19th Division is to attack and recapture DOIGNIES.

2. (a) The attack is to be carried out by 57th Inf. Bde. and one Coy. No.8 Tank Battalion. The British line, position of Deployment boundaries and objectives of the attack are shewn on the special map issued herewith to battalions.
Care is to be taken to form a defensive flank facing Northwards from DOIGNIES to BEAUMETZ.

(b) 58th Inf. Bde. is to entrench itself along the Ridge West of HERMIES as far as J.27 central.
Reserve Battalion of 57th Inf. Bde. is to continue this line towards BEAUMETZ.

3. 56th Inf. Bde. (less 1 Coy. 1/4th Shrops. L.I. now at E.17.a.9.3.) will be in Divisional Reserve and will assemble in GAIKA COPSE

4. Battalions will assemble at GAIKA Copse or in the vicinity if shelled as under:-

9th Ches. Regt. (on Right) In O.6.b.
8th N.Staff. Regt. (on Left) I.36.c.
1/4th Shrops. L.I. (less 1 Coy.) in O.6.a.

5. Battalions will move by Companies as soon as possible after receipt of this order.

6. 56th T.M.Bty. will remain in their present camp.

7. The attack is to be carried out in accordance with the orders of the G.O.C. 57th Inf. Bde. subject to the following:-

(a) Rates of advance will be from Position of Deployment to 3rd System - 100 yards in 2 minutes.
Pause of 3 minutes on clearing wire of 3rd System.
From outside wire of 3rd System to S.W. outskirts of DOIGNIES - 100 yards in 2 minutes.
From S.W. outskirts of DOIGNIES to 2nd System - Infantry follow the tanks making good the ground.

(b) A portion of the tanks are to move through DOIGNIES Village.

(c) At the moment when the Infantry and tanks leave the position of deployment the Field Artillery are to place a standing barrage on the S.W. edge of DOIGNIES and and arrangements are being made to put smoke on spur S.W. of BOURSIES, DOIGNIES and LOUVERVAL.

(d) 4 Machine Guns are allotted to 57th Inf. Bde. as forward guns for consolidation. Remainder of M.Gs. are to cover the advance with barrage fire.

(e) 94th Field Coy. R.E. and 1 Coy. Pioneers are attached to 57th Inf. Bde. 82nd Field Coy. R.E. and 1 coy. Pioneers to 58th Inf. Bde. These technical troops are to be used for consolidation.

8. Zero hour will be 7.0 p.m.

9. A synchronised watch will be sent round Battalions at 10.0 p.m. tonight.

10. First line transport will remain in its present location. Battalions will establish 2nd Echelon H.Q. in charge of an Officer.

11. H.Qs. will be as under:-

    57th Inf. Bde. - O.5.d.8.8. Advanced H.Q. at J.32.b.8.8.

    58th Inf. Bde. - O.5.c.8.8.

    56th Inf. Bde. - O.4.d.9.9.

12. Battalions will report by runner as soon as move is completed giving map location of Battalion H.Qs.

13. A Brigade Signal Station will be opened in GAIKA Copse at 9.0 p.m. This station will be connected with Bde. H.Q. (a) by visual (b) by wire.

14. ACKNOWLEDGE.

Issued at 7.45 p.m.

Bde. H.Q.
21st March 1918.
A.J.G.

                              Captain,
                         Brigade Major,
                56th Infantry Brigade.

Copies to:-

1. 19th Div. "G".
2. 19th Div. "Q".
3. 57th Inf. Bde.
4. 58th Inf. Bde.
5. 9th Ches. Regt.
6. 1/4th Shrops. L.I.
7. 8th N.Staff. Regt.
8. 55th T.M.Bty.
9. Signals.
10. R.A.
11. A.D.M.S.
12. G.O.C.
13. Staff Captain.
14. Bde. T.O.
15. War Diary.
16. File.

"A" Form.
MESSAGES AND SIGNALS.

Army Form C. 2121.

This message is on a/c of:
App J2/g

TO All Bns

Bm 475/S 21   AAA

Bde is to occupy the GREEN Line from I 28 central to the Bouzincourt Frenvillers Road about I 21 a 0.3 AAA Move takes place tonight aaa Detailed orders follow

From R X T
Time 10.20 Pm

APP J218

"C" Form.
MESSAGES AND SIGNALS.

Army Form C. 2123.

TO: All Btns

Sender's Number	Day of Month	In reply to Number	
Bm 470	21		AAA

Units will rendezvous at DELSAUX Farm as soon as possible aaa Detailed orders as to the occupation of the GREEN Line will be issued on arrival there aaa DELSAUX Farm is at J29a36

received 11.45.
Left Auned 12.15
arrived Delsaux
Farm 1.150

FROM
PLACE & TIME   11.30 p

56th Infantry Brigade No. B.M. 1157.

SECRET & URGENT.

All Battalions.
A Coy. 19th M.G.Bn.
56th T.M.Bty.
19th Div. "G". (for information).

---

1. Enemy are reported moving S. in I.5.c. and West along Main BAPAUME - CAMBRAI Road North of BEAUMETZ.

2. (a) 58th Inf. Bde. are to ensure junction with 51st Division about I.17.d.9.9.
   (b) 123rd Inf. Bde. (41st Division) are to take over the Front I.8.9. and 10. central to I.11.c. central during the night.
   (c) 58th Inf. Bde. are to hold BEUGNY and a line from I.17.d.9.9. to the road in I.10.c.8.8.

3. 56th Inf. Bde. is to extend its front Northwards taking over the GREEN (Army) Line up to I.14.b.8.0. (i.e. on the Southern grid of square I.14.b., which is now the Divisional boundary).

4. This re-adjustment will be carried out as under:-

   (a) 9th Ches. R. will take over from 8th N.Staff. R. portion of GREEN Line up to the ~~~~ at I.21.c.6.2. (inclusive to 9th Ches. R.)
   (b) 8th N.Staff. R. will sideslip to the Left and take over up to ~~~~ Bde. Left boundary. (It is not known whether this portion of the GREEN line is now occupied).
   (c) 8th N.Staff. R. will select a site for and establish a new Battn. H.Q. in a suitable position to command their new front.
   (d) Battalions will continue to hold the portions of the fronts allotted to them with three Coys. in the line and one Coy. in support. companies being dug in in depth.

5. A Coy. 19th Bn. M.G.Corps will move the battery of six guns from I.26.b. and will dispose of them so as to cover the new front with direct fire.

6. 56th T.M.Bty. will reconnoitre and select suitable defensive positions for 2 mortars in the new front and will occupy these when selected.

7. Moves will be completed as soon as possible.

8. Disposition reports will be forwarded to Bde. H.Q. by 8.30 a.m. today.

23rd March 1918.
A.J.G.

Captain,
Brigade Major,
56th Infantry Brigade.

56th Infantry Brigade No. S.G.662/Q.

App J22Q

All Battalions.
56th T.M.Bty.
A Company 19th Div. M.G. Bn.

In continuation of S.G.659/Q of today, the Grenade Dump has been established at I.28.a.0.1. It at present contains:-

      50 boxes S.A.A.
      20 " S.A.A. K.M. K.N. for M.Gs.
      40 " Mills Bombs.
      20 " Hales Grenades.
      750 1" Very Lights.
      30 S.O.S. Signals.
      120 Stokes Bombs.

The following additional stores will be delivered tonight:-

      150 boxes S.A.A.
      2000 Mills Grenades.
      100 boxes Hales Grenades.
      200 IV Corps S.O.S. Signals.

More Stokes Bombs will be delivered.

Units requiring Grenades etc. must draw them from the Dump.

Captain,
Staff Captain,
56th Infantry Brigade.

22nd March 1918.
A.J.G.

"A" Form.
MESSAGES AND SIGNALS.

Army Form C. 2121.

Prefix	Code	Words.	Charge.			
Office of Origin and Service Instructions		Sent At		This message is on a/c of: App J?? Service.	Reed. at Date	in.
Brigade R+TH		To By		(Signature of "Franking Officer.")	From By	

TO RXV

Sender's Number.	Day of Month.	In reply to Number.	
BM 557/3	23		A A A

In order to ensure touch with 6th Bde. on your right you will establish a liaison post in conjunction with the Latty on your right in the Green Line about I 28 Central as a Report when this has been done and the exact location of post

From
Place R+T 6Pn
Time

"B" Form.
MESSAGES AND SIGNALS.
Army Form C2122.

Office Stamp: App J222

TO: All Units & AA RA

Sender's Number: 52/5 Day of Month: 25

AAA

Indication point to enemy attacking on front I 34 B9.9 & BEUGNY

SECRET.   56th Infantry Brigade No.543/S.   App J223

All Units.

    Our Artillery will fire two barrages by way of counter preparation to-morrow morning, each lasting for fifteen minutes, i.e. 5.0 a.m. to 5.15 a.m., 6.15 to 6.30 a.m.

    Barrage in each case will start on S.O.S. Lines and creep backwards.

23rd March, 1918.   Captain,
   G.R.G.   Brigade Major,
                                              56th Infantry Brigade.

"A" Form
MESSAGES AND SIGNALS.

Army Form C. 2121 (in pads of 100).

App J224

TO: AXX RXV

Sender's Number.	Day of Month.	In reply to Number.	AAA
BM 550	24		

If compelled to withdraw from GREEN LINE 56 & 58 Bde will withdraw fighting through FREMICOURT and focus through RED LINE between BANCOURT and railway H28 B to trench system in square H33 SW of BAPAUME when troops will be reorganised. Addrs AXX RXV RXW Repeated 6th 57th 58th Brigades.

Place: RXT
Time: 11-50 AM

"A" Form.
MESSAGES AND SIGNALS.
Army Form C. 2121.
(In pads of 100.)

Prefix	Code	m	Words.	Charge.	This message is on a/c of:	Recd. at	m.
Office of Origin and Service Instructions.			Sent			Date	
			At	m.	D.R. Service.	From	
			To				
			By		(Signature of "Franking Officer.")	By	

TO OC. A. B. C. D. Coys.
    9/ K.S.L.I. 9 Cheshire
                 Regt. 11 I.B.

| Sender's Number. | Day of Month. | In reply to Number. | AAA |
| SR. 2 | 9/4 | | |

Be ready if compelled owing
to situation on RIGHT flank to
withdraw from GREEN Line following
via FREMICOURT and H.30 to
H.29 H.34 to H.33
The principle of the retirement
will be that two troops in
a support or reserve line will
hold their position until
they have covered the retirement
of and allowed all troops in
front of them to pass through
58th Brigade will withdraw
similarly N of CAMBRAI Road
As far as possible
retirement will be

From			
Place			
Time			

The above may be forwarded as now corrected. (Z)

Censor. Signature of Addressor or person authorised to telegraph in his name.
* This line should be erased if not required.

MESSAGES AND SIGNALS.   Army Form C. 2121.

opposed to usual attack formations commencing extended to West of FREMICOURT whence in artillery formation. Lead Battalion on a 3 Coy frontage. Each Coy on a two platoon frontage.

The right D Coy 8 ? Staffs will direct and march along Southern side of CAMBRAI Road. All stores etc. must be brought out. All Huts Camps Dumps etc. destroyed as troops pass them. This is extremely necessary so as to form a smoke screen to cover retirement.

All Vickers Guns will withdraw with that line which is nearest their present positions.

Bn HQ will precede the retirement of front line.

Acknowledge.

To A B C D Coys   App 3225/1/7

Be ready if compelled owing to situation on RIGHT flank to withdraw from GREEN line fighting via FREMICOURT and H 30 H 29 H 34 to H 38.

The principles of the retirement will be that no troops in a support or reserve line will vacate their position until they have covered the retirement of and allowed all troops in front of them to pass through. 58 Bde will withdraw similarly North of CAMBRAI

As far as possible retirement will be

opposite to usual attack formation
commencing extended order to WEST
of TREMICOURT and thence in Artillery formation Each Coy. on
a two platoon frontage - the
batt. on a ~~3~~ Company
frontage.

The left + "C" Company will
direct - and keep in well with
North Staffs on their present left.

All stores must be brought out.
All huts, camps, dug-outs etc
destroyed as troops pass thro'
This is especially necessary in
order to create the smoke barrage
as given to cover the men out.

Bn HQ will precede the retirement of the front line.
× Acknowledge ×

N.B. Arrangements must be
made now inconspicuously
for the withdrawal - which
will not take place until
absolutely necessary + a code
word from the Adjt B Coys. and
batt. be "BUCKSHEE" + 9 ..... Cost

"A" Form — Army Form C. 2121
MESSAGES AND SIGNALS. App J226

TO: 9 ches R
    1/ Shropshire R
    8 N Staff R

Sender's Number: B.M.2
Day of Month: 26
AAA

The Bde of the fourth Australian Division will take over from 19 Div the defence of HEBUTERNE. The relief will take place this evening. On relief 19 Division will withdraw to SAILLY-AU-BOIS — FONQUE VILLERS Road. 56 Inf Bde will take over the right sector from J.18.D.5.0. to the CHATEAU-DE-LA HAYE — HEBUTERNE Rd exclusive. 5) Inf Bde on the left from to E.27.D central. 58 Inf Bde will be in reserve in BAYENCOURT. Posts will be established by the right Bde at J.24.A central and J.24.B.8.6. and

"A" Form
MESSAGES AND SIGNALS.   Army Form C. 2121

J.27.A Central and by left O.ste at K.8.B.2.6. and K.7.D.9.9. Bde HQ will be at BAYENCOURT. Battalions will be disposed as follows:-

Right. 8 N. Staff R. will be accommodated in the village west of the grid line running N & S through J.18 and be responsible for the defence of the Southern and Western outskirts of the village and will furnish posts of one N.C.O. and six men at J.23.A.9.9. and

"A" Form
MESSAGES AND SIGNALS.   Army Form C. 2121
                              (in pads of 100).
                              No. of Message..........

Prefix......Code......m.	Words	Charge.		
Office of Origin and Service Instructions.			This message is on a/c of	Recd. at......m.
	Sent			Date........
At......m			Service.	
To				From........
By		Signature of "Franking Officer."	By........

TO | | III | |

| Sender's Number. | Day of Month. | In reply to Number. | AAA |

To A.3.5.

Order to troops .5 will be
responsible for the southern
and eastern portion of
54/24? as far as K.7.c.3.6.
and that at J.26.B.9.6. and
will be accommodated in the
eastern side of the village.
left. & the R. responsible to
hold from K.7.c.3.6. to
[illegible] — [illegible] to
[illegible] & Bat. troops and
will be accommodated in the
northern portion of the village
starts out take at there new position.

From			
Place			
Time			

The above may be forwarded as now corrected.   (Z)

Censor........ Signature of Addressor or person authorised to telegraph in his name
* This line should be erased if not required.
W¹. W493 M1647 100,000 pads. 4/17. W. & Co., Ltd. (E, 1197.)

"A" Form
MESSAGES AND SIGNALS.

of the village.
Units will send guides for
rations to SAILLY CHURCH
at 9.0 pm

From: 56 Inf Bde
Place:
Time: 8.0 am

[Signature] Bde Major

"A" Form
MESSAGES AND SIGNALS.

TO: All Battns & 56th TMBty

Sender's Number.	Day of Month.	In reply to Number.	
BMG 848	27/3/18		AAA

Battns must be prepared to fall in at short notice as the Situation is still critical and the enemy may break through between EUSTON DUMP (K.33.a) and HEBUTERNE men must not leave the vicinity of billets AAA Ammunition should be made up to 170 Rds per man AAA There is a Dump at K.33 a.2.8. AAA The Sectors allotted for the Defence of the village will remain the same as

"A" Form
MESSAGES AND SIGNALS.

Prefix... Code...m.	Words	Charge			
Office of Origin and Service Instructions.			This message is on a/c of		Recd. at......m.
	Sent				Date.........
	At.........m.		.........Service.		From
	To				
	By		Signature of "Franking Officer."	By	

TO {

| Sender's Number. | Day of Month. | In reply to Number. | AAA |

laid down in Bm. 2 except that the 9/Ches. R. might be required to move to J. my Pt to secure the right flank.

Should ~~this~~ necessity arise Lt. Col OAKEYNE will take command and issue orders direct to Battns without reference to the Brigade.

From: 56 Inf Bde
Place:
Time:

The above may be forwarded as now corrected.   (Z)   [signature] Capt

Censor.   Signature of Addressee or person authorised to telegraph in his name

* This line should be erased if not required.
Wt. W402/M1047 100,000 pads. 4/17. W. & Co., Ltd. (E. 1187.)

SECRET   56TH. Infantry Brigade Order No. 116   COPY No. 1

Reference LENS 11 1/100,000

1. 19th. Division is being withdrawn and transferred to the ST.OMER area.

2. 56th. Inf. Bde. group consisting of 3 Battalions, 81st. Field Coy. R.E., 56th. T.M.Bty., and 5/S.W.Borderers will move to THIEVRES to-day by march route in accordance with the attached march table.

3. 1st. Line Transport of Battalions less that required to move kit etc. from SAILLY will march under the orders of Bde. Transport Officer

4. Billeting parties consisting of 1 Officer and 5 O.Rs. per battalion and other units as required will report at Bde. H.Q. at 9 a.m. to proceed by lorry, except parties of 81st. Field Coy. R.E. which will proceed direct.

5. 1 lorry will report at SAILLY CHURCH at 12 noon and proceed to THIEVRES via BAYENCOURT to pick up stragglers.

6. Brigade H.Q. will close at BAYENCOURT at 10 a.m. and re-open at THIEVRES at the same hour.

7. ACKNOWLEDGE.

Issued at 3.30.A.M.

Bde. H.Q.
March 28th, 1918.
A.V.E.

Captain,
A/Brigade Major,
56th. Infantry Brigade.

Copies to:-

1. 9/Ches.R.
2. 1/4th. Shrops.L.I.
3. 8/N.Staffs.R.
4. 56th. T.M.Bty.
5. Bde TO
6. 81st. Fld. Coy. R.E.
7. 19th. Division "G"
8. 19th. Division
9. A.D.M.S.
10. C.R.E.
11. A.P.M.
12. 57th. Inf. bde.
13. 58th. Inf. bde.
14. G.O.C.
15. Staff Captain
16. War Diary.
17. File.

Copy to all recipients of C.O. No.116.
56th Infantry Brigade No.B.M.1177.

The destination of 56th Inf. Bde group is now FAMECHON and not THIEVRES.

Route via THIEVRES for Units from CAILLY and BAYENCOURT.

28th March, 1918.
C.R.G.

Captain,
Brigade Major,
56th Infantry Brigade.

MARCH TABLE.

Unit.	From	To	Starting Point	Time	Route	Remarks.
9/Ches.R.	SAILLY	THIEVRES / FAMECHON	Road junction West of SAILLY Church	2.0 p.m.	COIGNIEUX - ST. LEGER - AUTHIE	
1/4th. Shrops.L.I.	SAILLY	THIEVRES	-do-	2.5 p.m.	-do-	
8/N.Staffs.R.	SAILLY	THIEVRES	-do-	2.10 p.m.	-do-	
56th. T.M.Bty.	HENU	THIEVRES	Billets	2.0 p.m.	PAS - FAMECHON	
81st. Field Coy. R.E. LA Gauchie		THIEVRES	Billets	2.0 p.m.	GUADIEMPRE - PAS - Famechon	
5/S.B.Borderers.	LAVENCOURT	THIEVRES	Billets	2.25 p.m.	COIGNIEUX - ST. LEGER - AUTHIE	
Transport.	HENU	THIEVRES	Billets	2.5 p.m.	PAS - FAMECHON	

Copy No   9th Bn Cheshire Regt Order No 14
                                              28-3-18
Ref Map LENS 11. 1/100,000

1. The 56th Inf Brigade moves to THIEVRES today 28th March 1918.

2. The Battalion will move from BAILLY to THIEVRES by route march via COIGNEUX - ST LEGER - AUTHIE.

(a) ORDER Companies will parade in time to move off at 2.pm at 100 yds distance in the order
   HQ, A. B. C. D.

(b) DRESS Fighting Order, blankets to be carried rolled inside the ground sheet & tied horseshoe round the haversack. Steel helmets are to be clean.
   Men will carry the ordinary complement of S.A.A. All surplus will be handed in to the R.S.M.

(c) Camp Kettles, officers spare kits and any surplus stores will be carried on the S.A.A. limber which must be packed by 1.p.m. This will follow in rear of the Battalion.

3. Brigade HQ will close at BAYENCOURT at 1.p.m and open at THIEVRES at the same time

Copies to 1. CO   6 RSM
         2. A   7 MO
         3. B   8 File
         4. C
         5. D

                              Capt
                    Adjt 9th Bn Cheshire Regt

56th Infantry Brigade No. B.M. 1173

App J229

All Units.

      The following Wire No. GA 720 of the 28th received from 19th Division:-

      "Divl. Commander will watch Brigade on the march today from a point just E. of COIGNEUX."

28th March, 1918.
G.R.G.

                    Captain,
              A/ Brigade Major,
           56th Infantry Brigade.

SECRET   WD   COPY No. 1.

56th Infantry Brigade Order No. 117.

App J30

Reference
   LENS 11 - 1/100,000
   HAZEBROUCK 5A - 1/100,000.

1. The 19th Division will be transferred by Rail from the 3rd to 2nd Army.

2. The 56th Inf. Bde. group complete with all Horse Transport will move by Rail from CANAS to CAESTRE tomorrow, in accordance with the attached Train Table.

3. Units will march to the entraining Station in accordance with the attached March Table.

4. Baggage and Supply wagons will entrain with Units.

5. Entraining and detraining Officers and loading parties will be detailed in accordance with the attached table.

6. All food and forage required for journey must be put in carriages and trucks.

7. Transport will arrive at entraining station three hours and personnel 1½ hours before ~~commencement of entraining~~ *departure of the train.*

8. Marching out states for all Units must be handed in to R.T.Os. at entraining Stations.

9. Units must supply drag ropes for horse trucks.

10. Units will detail an Officers to proceed to the entraining station to reconnoitre approaches etc. before the arrival of the units. This Officer should bring an entraining state with him

11. (a) All trains consist of 1 Officer's carriage; 17 flat trucks; 30 covered trucks.
   (b) (i) Each flat truck will take an average of 4 axles.
      (ii) Each covered truck will take 6 H.D.Horses, or 8 L.D.Horses or mules, or 40 men.
   (c) No personnel or stores will be allowed in the brake vans at each end of the train, or on the roofs of the trucks. No covered trucks should be used for baggage as it restricts space for personnel.

12. SUPPLY ARRANGEMENTS.
   (i) Supply wagons of Train will deliver rations for consumption 29th instant, to units on 28th instant. They will return to the Divisional Train Camp at MONDICOURT and load up with rations for consumption 30th instant. The supply wagons will then return to units and entrain with them loaded.
   (ii) Rations for consumption March 31st will be dumped at refilling point in the new area on the 30th instant and the location of these R. Ps. will be notified to units as they detrain.
   (iii) Refilling on 30th in the new area will be at 3.0. p.m, and units will send guides to the R. Ps. notified.

13. Guides will meet units at the detraining station and conduct them to their Billets.

14. Times of departure of trains and time units are to pass the starting points will be notified later.

15. ACKNOWLEDGE.

Issued at

Brigade H.Q.
28-3-18.

                                            Captain,
                                      A/Brigade Major,
                                  56th Infantry Brigade.

Copies to :-

1. 9th Ches. R.
2. 1/4th Shrops. L.I.
3. 5th N.Staff. R.
4. 56th T.M.Bty.
5. 57th Field Amb.
6. 81st Field Co. R.E.
7. No. 2 Co. 19th Div. Train.
8. T.O.7th R.Lanc.R.
9. 19th Div. "Q".
10. 19th Div. "Q".
11. D.M.G.O.
12. A.D.M.S.
13. C.R.E.
14. A.P.M.
15. 57th Inf. Bde.
16. 58th Inf. Bde.
17. G.O.C.
18. Staff Captain.
19. Brigade T.O.
20. Signals.
21. War Diary.
22. File.
23. Spare.

MARCH TABLE.

Schedule Number.	Unit.	Starting point.	Route.	Time.	Remarks.
1.	6/Ches.R.(less 1 Coy.with Cooker and Water Cart.	South West exit to PAIECHON.	THIEVRES - ORVILLE - ALPLIER FRESCHEVILLERS DOULLENS.		Transport will pass the starting point 1½ hours before the time stated for personnel.
2.	53th Bde. H.Q.	ditto.	ditto.		ditto.
3.	55th T.M.Bty.	ditto.	ditto.		ditto.
4.	1 Coy.S/Shes.R. with Cooker and Water Cart.	ditto.	ditto.		ditto.
5.	1/4 Shrops.L.I. (less 1 Coy.with Cooker and Water Cart).	ditto.	ditto.		ditto.
6.	8/N.Sts.f.R.(less 1 Coy.with Cooker and Water Cart).	ditto.	ditto.		ditto.
7.	57th F.A.	Billets.	LUCHEUX - DOULLENS.		ditto.
8.	1 Coy.8/N.Staff.R. with Cooker and Water Cart.	South West exit to FAMECHON.	THIEVRES - SARTON - FRESCHEVILLERS - DOULLENS.		ditto.
9.	31st Field Co.R.E.	S.W.exit to FAMECHON.	ditto.		ditto.
10.	No.2 Co.Div.Train.	Billets.	DOULLENS.		
11.	5th S.A.A.	S.W.exit to FAMECHON.	THIEVRES - SARTON - FRESCHEVILLERS - DOULLENS.		Transport will pass the starting point 1½ hours before the time stated for personnel.

Schedule Number.	Unit.	Starting point.	Route.	Time.	Remarks.
12.	Transport 7/R. Lanc. R.	S.W. exit to FALECHON.	THIEVRES - SARTON - FALSCHVILLERS - DOULLENS.		
13.	"A" Coy. 18th Div. M. G. Batn.	Billets.	HALLOY - AMPLIER - DOULLENS.		Transport will pass the starting point 1½ hours before the times for personnel.

ENTRAINING TABLE.

Train No.	Entraining Station.	Date.	Time.	Unit.
1.	CANDAS.	29-3-18.		9/Ches.R.(less 1 Coy. with Cooker and Water Cart), Transport 7/R.Lanc.R.
2.	CANDAS.			56th Bde. H.Q. 56th T.M.Bty. Sig. Section. "A" Coy. 19th M.G.Bn. 1 Coy. 9/Ches.R. with Cooker and Water Cart.
3.	CANDAS.			1/4th Shrops. L.I. (less 1 Coy. with Cooker and Water Cart).
4.	CANDAS.			6/N.Staff.R. (less 1 Coy. with Cooker and Water Cart).
5.	CANDAS.			57th Field Amb. H.Q.Div. Train. 1 Coy. 1/4th Shrops. L.I. with Cooker and Water Cart. 1 Coy. 6/N.Staff.R. with Cooker and Water Cart
6.	CANDAS.			81st Field Co. R.E. No. 2 Co. Div. Train.
7.	CANDAS.			5th S.Wales Bord. (P.)

Table of personnel to be detailed
by Units at entraining and
detraining stations.

nit.	Officers.	O. R.	Duties.	Remarks.
/4th Shrops.L.I.	2	-	Assist R.T.O. at entraining station.	Report 4 hours before departure of first train.
/4th Shrops.L.I.	2	-	Assist R.T.O. at detraining station.	Depart by first train and report to R.T.O. on arrival.
/N.Staff.R.	2	100	Loading	Report 4 hours before departure of No. 1 Train. Depart by train No. 9 with 1 Cooker and 1 Water Cart to accompany.
/Ches.R.	2	100	Unloading	Depart by No. 1 Train reporting to R.T.O. at detraining station. 1 Cooker and 1 Water Cart to accompany.

All the above will be rationed for consumption 29th and 30th inst. Cookers and Water Carts supplied as above will also be for use of 58th Inf, de. parties.

56th Infantry Brigade No. O.O.117/1.

All recipients of O.O.117.

1. Reference O.O.117.
   Trains leave CANDAS Station at the following hours:-
   Train No. 1 at 9. 0. a.m.
   "   "   2 "12. 0. noon.
   "   "   3 " 3. 0. p.m.
   "   "   4 " 6. 0. p.m.
   "   "   5 " 9. 0. p.m.
   "   "   6 "12. 0. midnight.
   "   "   7 " 3. 0 a.m. 30th inst.

2. Units will pass the starting point laid down in the March Table (to which Schedule numbers refer) as below:-
   Schedule No. 1 at 2.30 a.m.
   "   "   2 " 5.30 a.m.
   "   "   3 " 5.35 a.m.
   "   "   4 " 5.40 a.m.
   "   "   5 " 8.30 a.m.
   "   "   6 " ~~12.00 p.m.~~ 11.30 p.m.
   "   "   7 " 1.45 p.m.
   "   "   8 " 2.30 p.m.
   "   "   9 " 3.30 p.m.
   "   "   10 " 4.0 p.m.
   "   "   11 " 8.30 p.m.
   "   "   12 " 1.30 a.m.
   "   "   13 " 5.30 a.m.

29th March, 1918.
G.R.G.

Captain,
A/Brigade Major,
56th Infantry Brigade.

"A" Form
MESSAGES AND SIGNALS.

TO: 9 Ches R

Sender's Number: BM.8
Day of Month: 29
AAA

Reference OO 11) information just received that your train leaves CANDAS at 9.0 am today aaa your transport should move off at once and personnel should proceed starting first at 2.30 am aaa Train for your odd coy leaves at 12 noon aaa telephly

Place: 56 Inf Bde

56th Brigade.
19th Division.

1/9th BATTALION

THE CHESHIRE REGIMENT

APRIL 1918.

Army Form C. 2118.

WAR DIARY
or
INTELLIGENCE SUMMARY.
(Erase heading not required.)

Instructions regarding War Diaries and Intelligence Summaries are contained in F. S. Regs., Part II. and the Staff Manual respectively. Title pages will be prepared in manuscript.

Place	Date	Hour	Summary of Events and Information	Remarks and references to Appendices
Fauquissart Cerny (N21.C.0.5 Sheet 36SW)	1919 April 1		The Brigade was inspected by the G.O.C. II Army who complimented	Appx 1
			them on the good work done in the south.	
			Reconnaissance and General Order No 118 and Battn Order No 5 Re	K2
			Battalion move to new Camp issued WARGHEM (T.6 central)	
	2		Rest. This move was completed by 2.16 pm	
			Training and resting. Baths	
	3		On accordance with Indoor Orders a reconnaissance of the Corps	K3
			line was carried out by officers concerned. The Divisional Comm-	
			ander the N Corps a.m. 1 p.m to a.m. 26 O.R. reinforcements arrived	K4
	4		Training	
	5		A working party of 1 officer and 56 men was supplied for work on K5	
			on the Corps Front and an early relay was provided Divisional to	K6
			and including the O.C Corps. E OR reinforcements arrived.	
	6		ditto	

WAR DIARY
or
INTELLIGENCE SUMMARY.
(Erase heading not required.)

Army Form C. 2118.

Place	Date	Hour	Summary of Events and Information	Remarks and references to Appendices
T.S. Central (Sheet 28 N.W.)	1918 April		In accordance with Brigade Order No.119 and Batt. Order No.6 the Battalion moved off at 2.30 p.m. to ROSSIGNOL Camp. En route however verbal orders were received from Brigade that the move was cancelled and would not take place until the following morning. The Battalion returned to former Camps & O.R. reinforcement arrivals.	App. K.7.
	8		Parties reconnoitred the line in the left sub-sector frontage. Oh	" K.8.
		11.30 a.m.	The Battalion moved off for ROSSIGNOL Camp. N.21.6.91. Sheet 28) where it was billeted by 1.50 p.m. Capt J.H. DRESSER, and 331 O.R. being then under command.	" K.9.
ROSSIGNOL Camp (N.29.6.9.1)	9		The warning orders contained in para 3 of Brigade Order No.110 (app K.9) that 56th Brigade would relieve the 5th Brigade and the MESSINES Sector on the night of 9th/10th April was cancelled and called " K.10 other orders reference this relief. Warning orders were received about 4.45 p.m. that Battalion arrivals must to MAVESYRES write 10h not. Also verbal orders were received to be ready to move at half an hours notice - These orders once communicated to companies. Capt. was later confirmed in writing by Brigade about 11.30 p.m.	" K.11 " K.12

WAR DIARY or INTELLIGENCE SUMMARY

Army Form C. 2118.

Place	Date	Hour	Summary of Events and Information	Remarks and references to Appendices
ROSSIGNOL CAMP (Nr. Rouen)	1918 April 9		verbal orders were issued by Brigade on the evening that the Battalion would move to DIEPPE. by motor bus. Three orders were issued.	Appx. 13
			Communicated to Companies. The Battalion was attached to the 102nd Inf. Brigade of the 74th Division. And an officer/man/driver was detailed to report to this Brigade HQ immediately on arrival.	K. 14
			Confirmation of the verbal orders were received. gun teams Sec. No. 2.	K. 15
			The Lewis Gun Section Gun Teams Kennels about Tanks and anti-acks.	
	10		Transit could use his stores were loaned and ammunition to the Priestman lines. By H. of Brigade Buses had arrived by Entrus the Battalion arrived at Rendezvous off at 5 a.m. leaving the desk two reserved (Officers and 147 O.R./below men in charge	
			of 3 men.) Preserving the only officer left out of action. The following transfered off with the Battalion — Commanding Lt-Col. G. K. FULTON. Regiment Captain E. GRAVES. Signalling Officer. Lieut. D. SILCOCK. Medical Off. Capt.	
			Lieut. A WALKER. " " Lieut. G. DNAYER (arms). Capt. H. DRESSER. Lieut. A. E. INGHBOGGE. R. Cov. " " Capt. W.H. BARNES (armoury) Lieut. A. BAIRD.	

WAR DIARY
or
INTELLIGENCE SUMMARY.

(Erase heading not required.)

Army Form C. 2118.

Place	Date	Hour	Summary of Events and Information	Remarks and references to Appendices
	1/1/17 17 April	10		
NIEPPE B.43.r.6 (sheet 36)			C. Coy. Capt. ARNOLTON Coy: 2nd Lt WILKINSON. D. Coy: 2nd Lt V.E. HUMPHRIES Coy: 2nd Lt A. THORNE. Total 12 Officers 752 Other Ranks. The Battalion duly arrived in NIEPPE and was billeted by 6.50 a.m. The village was somewhat damaged by heavy long range shell fire, and was still occasionally receiving attention from the enemy M.V. guns. It was soon learned that the enemy had attacked on a front extending from the front of PLOEGSTEERT WOOD to South of ARMENTIERES. The officer's already detailed for the purpose reported to the 102nd Inf. Brigade H.Q. and the Commanding Officer also accompanied them to learn the situation and obtain orders. Before he returned orders were received from the 154th Inf Brigade that the battalion had been placed under the orders of that brigade. Instant Orders were issued by the Brigade Major for the battalion to take up a line D.2 of NIEPPE along the road through CI3.C.9 and CI (sheet 33) This was duly done and was completed by about 2 p.m. - two Companies being in support	App. K.16 App. K.17

WAR DIARY or INTELLIGENCE SUMMARY.

Army Form C. 2118.

Place	Date	Hour	Summary of Events and Information	Remarks and references to Appendices
NIEPPE L.C. K16 L.C. K22	1918 April 10		line and was support. The situations were unquiet and disorganised. During the afternoon and at 4 P.M. were augmented in C.H.3 (App. K.18). By this time the enemy's attacking force had succeeded in forcing their way through into PLOEGSTEERT WOOD and were taking the troops in front of the battalion in the rear. Three troops fell back fighting into the battalion line and by 4.30 p.m. the enemy was decided by our left front Company/Cotts. HQ was established at COURTE RUE – B.Qd – and forwards HQ at TROIS App.K.18.	
COURTE RUE (in Shed 36)			Bois T.30.6) by ensuring to enemy successes in bringing up guns and was shelling the front companies fairly heavily – he also twice attacked, both these attacks were repulsed owing to the situation on the flanks, especially on the right flank where the enemy who reported to have captured STEENWERCKS – it was necessary to withdraw the front line and in conformity with other units and according to Brigade Order No B.H.F. 23 the battalion withdrew its front line to round OESTHOVER. 0.8.c.5.3.2. (Sheet 36) App K.19.	

WAR DIARY
or
INTELLIGENCE SUMMARY.
(Erase heading not required.)

Army Form C. 2118.

Place	Date	Hour	Summary of Events and Information	Remarks and references to Appendices
COURCELLE (B.10. d.9.3.)	11		and touch was obtained with the battalion of the 1st Brigade on the right and the 8th Yorks Regt on the left. This was completed by 3.30 a.m. At 6 a.m. rations were received. The kitchens and cooks getting clear just before the enemy shelling commenced in earnest. Section teams over the whole battalion area. The enemy also commenced the active artillery attack was expected. At 11.25 a.m. an enemy aeroplane was brought down by rifle and Lewis Gun fire of the battalion. About 8.30 a.m. enemy fire increased and his troops were seen moving about by it, preparing to launch an attack. At 10 a.m. his fire had increased to a barrage and at 10.30 a.m. he delivered a small attack, this was repulsed with heavy loss him on the battalion front but succeeded in forcing our early out to the right of the line (approx. the front line companies were withdrawn to the Army Line (Sunken Road) extending from B.10 and B.12 west 3) between at 4 p.m. was on HEBUTERNE (ap. K.21) — the trench 7.20	App. K.20

WAR DIARY or INTELLIGENCE SUMMARY

Army Form C. 2118.

Place	Date	Hour	Summary of Events and Information	Remarks and references to Appendices
COURTE RUE (S.10 sheet 36)	11		Continuously during the left front, which was gradually being forced in and the 15th Brigade becoming the forward point of a "bottle neck" salient. During the afternoon the enemy subjected the Battalion's position to very heavy shell fire and several times attempted to send forward small attacking parties, these were successfully dealt off. About 1pm an enemy M.G. post was located by the Commanding Officer to be in the buildings at BRUNE CAYE and was bringing enfilade fire to bear on our position. A party was sent to turn the enemy out. The party consisted of 1 Officer (Capt.) STRONG and 20 men of the 8th BORDER Regt. and 10 men and 1 N.C.O. of the Yorkshire who partly surrounded the building capturing some 10 men and 10 Officers. 14 other ranks were taken prisoner. The pretto Officer was wounded. During the day the position Casualties had not been heavy, with Lieut. W. BARNES being killed about 10.30 am and Capt. J. NABOR shortly afterwards before the unit moved to the ARMY LINE, sundries suffering casualties back.	App K.21

WAR DIARY
or
INTELLIGENCE SUMMARY.

Army Form C. 2118.

Place	Date	Hour	Summary of Events and Information	Remarks and references to Appendices
Croix Rut (B 10 Sqd 3)	1918 April 11		increased – the position becoming almost untenable about 4.30 p.m. being heavily shelled from all directions (it was comparable to hell) & our own Artillery was shooting short but apparences were strongly in favour of this. Casualties to other ranks during the day were estimated at 150. The enemy again put down an exceedingly heavy barrage at 7 p.m. and his infantry attacked about 7.40 – This attack completely broke down under our rifle and Machine Gun fire. At 7.30 p.m. orders were received that the Rossignol Salient was to be evacuated at 10.30 p.m. So it was specially light and the enemy was now about advancing heavily with his machine guns, it was impracticable to commence with the withdrawal until 8.15 p.m. at which time the Battalion Commenced its withdrawal, some element of the troops on the Battalion's left had already withdrawn, however, and we had two Companies facing to flank. They got out by 11.30 p.m. two Companies and Battn HQ were established a line at B.3.a.7.4 (the Brigade having	Apps K2 &

Army Form C. 2118.

WAR DIARY
or
INTELLIGENCE SUMMARY.
(Erase heading not required.)

Instructions regarding War Diaries and Intelligence Summaries are contained in F. S. Regs., Part II. and the Staff Manual respectively. Title pages will be prepared in manuscript.

Place	Date	Hour	Summary of Events and Information	Remarks and references to Appendices
EMPERNISSE FARM (5.3. Sheet 36)	April 11		Had orders to side-slip on arrival at PONT D'ACHELLES and went	
			straight on infront of HAMPERNISSE FARM. About midnight the other two companies B+C arrived and took up positions in this line.	
			Sergt. V.E. HUMPHRIES was reported missing as from the early morning of the 11th after this was advanced but eventually found at no. hospital wounded. Capt A.K. WALTON was wounded by a sniper from LAROMAIN	
			About 4.30 p.m. except for occasional shots the remainder of the night passed quietly. The enemy's very lights could be seen however gradually drawing closer. About 10 a.m. he had been beaten in the upper end of R. Centaals (sheet 36) and movement in this direction attracted the fire of snipers. Shelling increased from 6 a.m. onwards	
	12		No further enemy was seen on the battalion front except an occasional solitary man both were seen in large numbers on our right rear around the NEPPE - BAILLEUL Road. At 10.40 a.m. he was seen to bring field guns out of NEPPE in a gallop over	
			Got iron rods about B.Q.C. see situation report - Apx K 23	Apx K 23

WAR DIARY
or
INTELLIGENCE SUMMARY.
(Erase heading not required.)

Army Form C. 2118.

Place	Date	Hour	Summary of Events and Information	Remarks and references to Appendices
LONKERWISSE	1915 April 12		A Battalion of the MONMOUTHS on our right suffered heavily from these guns and from Trench Mortars. At 4.30 p.m the enemy (who had since that morning two troops) delivered an attack astride the BARRIER Road and broke through the Battalion's right. No reinforcements coming to the MONMOUTHS and there were no troops to reinforce the right flank, sharp enfilade fire was being opened on the battalion from the S side of the road. It was decided therefore to withdraw on to the high ground around NEUVE EGLISE which was strongly occupied by Machine Guns. During the night a general withdrawal of the Brigade was supported.	
RAVELSBURG	13		was ordered. A new line NEUVE EGLISE – RAVELSBURG – MONT DE LILLE. The present frontage being T.w c 3.5 to 51/4.a central. This was held by two battalions in the front line, the 9th Cheshire being on the right. Battalion H.Q. was established at S.16.b.6.u. Shelling on a small cottage. The alarm was very minor. At 6 a.m enemy shelling commenced and by 9 a.m was most violent, especially	

WAR DIARY
or
INTELLIGENCE SUMMARY.
(Erase heading not required.)

Army Form C. 2118.

Place	Date	Hour	Summary of Events and Information	Remarks and references to Appendices
RAVELSBERG	1914 Apl 13		in the neighbourhood of the BAILLEUL main road (from ARMENTIERES) - No infantry action appeared to follow however but the morning was too much. It was impossible to see more than 50 yards. 10 A.M. the situation was again quiet and by 1 P.M. scarce a sound could be heard. 7.30 P.M. the front line was driven in about 8.20 - enemy lights could be seen gradually drawing nearer from a southerly direction until in the neighbourhood of WEST OF FARM Cross "TROIS ROIS CABARET" the night however passed quietly and our ascendancy was made by the 4th Brigade to establish a line along road CRUCIFIX CORNER - AU TROIS ROIS.	
	14		At dawn however the enemy attacked along the valley WATERLOO Road and broke in up the re-entrant to LEWIS FARM. Most effective fire was however brought to bear upon troops in T.B.C. and S.I8. as from the Battalion position in S.18 a & b and heavy losses inflicted on him. Severe & severe fighting ensued however in	

WAR DIARY
or
INTELLIGENCE SUMMARY.

Army Form C. 2118.

Place	Date	Hour	Summary of Events and Information	Remarks and references to Appendices
RYVELSBURG	14		The neighbourhood of BRAEMEERSCHEN (S.R.C.) in which Lt.Col. G.K. FULTON was killed. The enemy was driven off the hill about LEWIS FARM by a counter attack by the — to the N Fusiliers, who captured 100 prisoners were brought in. Direct communication was obtained with the artillery from Battn H.Q. and most effective shelling was carried out on WESTHOF FARM – T.19 – T.25 – T.30, which caused the enemy's casualties to be enormous. The situation at 6.30 a.m. was as stated on CHQ 92 (Capp. K.24) from about 9 am App.124. 5.4 pm the day passed quietly except for occasional shelling of our position and heavy fire on the rear areas by the enemy. Capt H.J. DRESSER assumed Command temporarily. At 4.30 pm the enemy attacked in mass from NEUVE EGLISE to the main BAILLEUL – ARMENTIERES road and one N through NEUVE EGLISE. The barrage opened at 4 pm and was very heavy from the commanding position held by the remaining men of the Battalion they were able to inflict many casualties on the	

WAR DIARY or INTELLIGENCE SUMMARY

Army Form C. 2118.

Place	Date	Hour	Summary of Events and Information	Remarks and references to Appendices
	1916 Appx	11	enemy by rifle and machine gun fire on his troops attacking on both flanks - inspite of enemy's barrage fire. The situation on the right could not be obtained from our position but on the left the attack deemed to be very successful. About 1 pm however our artillery fired down on Palenche barrage. Eventhough our infantry turned and ran, arms in hand the situation became I has been reported. The night passed in fairly quietly. At 12.15 a.m orders were received that the battalion should be relieved by the 1st MANCHESTER Regt of the 6th Brigade. Relief was duly carried out and the Battalion marched out to DRANOUTRE at 3 a.m. to the rest bivouacs. Travelled through 5 Officers, 201 O.ranks. On arrival at this	App K25
KOUDOKOT	13		point the battalion was met by guides and taken to KOUDOKOT (M.34.d Sheet 28) which it reached about 5 a.m. a hot meal was served and the men sent to rest in huts. At 2 pm the 15th Brigade moved off in accordance with B.F.51 (App K28)	App K26

WAR DIARY
or
INTELLIGENCE SUMMARY.
(Erase heading not required.)

Army Form C. 2118

Place	Date	Hour	Summary of Events and Information	Remarks and references to Appendices
KOUDOROT	1918 April 15		and orders were issued to the 9th Cheshire branch to KEMMEL SHELTERS and rejoin the 8th Inf. Brigade. The Battalion accordingly moved off at 2.15 p.m. and reached KEMMEL Shelters at 3.30 p.m. The enemy was shelling this area lightly and shell fell amongst one of the Companies and wounded Bran shortly after this orders were received that the Battalion would relieve a part of the KEMMEL Defences in the support line and be under the orders of the G.O.C 2nd Inf. Brigade. This position was reconnoitred by the Commanding Officer and the positions duly occupied by the Battalion. A & E Coys being on the front line and C & D Coys in the support line of this system. During the night the front line withdrew to the front line of this system.	App. K.28
KEMMEL DEFENCES	16		The enemy following up this withdrawal commenced a heavy shoot on the KEMMEL Defences and Hill at 9 a.m. This lasted until 3 p.m. the remainder of the day and night proved quiet. Orders were received that the Battalion could move to order	App. K.29

A6945 Wt. W14422/M1160. 350,000 12/16 D. D. & L. Forms/C/2118/14.

WAR DIARY
or
INTELLIGENCE SUMMARY.
(Erase heading not required.)

Army Form C. 2118.

Instructions regarding War Diaries and Intelligence Summaries are contained in F. S. Regs., Part II. and the Staff Manual respectively. Title pages will be prepared in manuscript.

Place	Date	Hour	Summary of Events and Information	Remarks and references to Appendices
KEPPEL DIVISIONAL DEFENCES	April 16		of the G.O.C. 58th Inf. Brigade once again. About dusk, our advanced parties of French troops began to arrive in the Battalion area to reconnoitre the position. A heavy barrage by the enemy	
	17		began again about 9 a.m on the 17th over the whole area and was more violent than ever. Gas shells were thrown and the Troops were compelled to wear their respirators for sometime. The barrage then lasted until 1 p.m. Casualties caused by the barrage were 3 O. Ranks. No infantry action appeared. The Battalion were 30 O.Ranks. No infantry action appeared & have followed, although the situation was obscure to its flanks. A warning order was received that the Division was to be relieved by the 25th French Division on the night 18/19th April. Ap 30	
	18		The afternoon and night passed quietly. At 4.30 a.m the enemy again put down a heavy barrage which lasted until 11 a.m. but no infantry action apparently followed on the Brigade front, but observation was very poor from 9 a.m. Our own artillery fired on the points were most active units.	

WAR DIARY or INTELLIGENCE SUMMARY.

Army Form C. 2118.

(Erase heading not required.)

Instructions regarding War Diaries and Intelligence Summaries are contained in F. S. Regs., Part II. and the Staff Manual respectively. Title pages will be prepared in manuscript.

Place	Date	Hour	Summary of Events and Information	Remarks and references to Appendices
KEMMEL	April 1915 13		about 1115 a.m. Direction fire became difficult except for desultory shelling by both sides, no concentrated shoot was carried out however by the enemy until 4 p.m. when a heavy barrage was again put down and his infantry endeavoured to attack – this attack was beaten back with heavy losses to enemy. About 4.30 p.m. definite news (App. K3) was received for the relief by the French. The evening and night passed quietly & the relief was slowly carried out, this was consequently hindered owing to the weakness and the difficulties of internalization.	App. K31
	14		by 5 a.m. however all positions of the Battalion had been occupied by the French troops and the Batten. moved off in accordance with forecable instructions and Batten Order 108 (App. K31) and assembled in M.l.b. Ronchow. The march was continued to billets in WIPPENHOEK L.25. Sheet 27, which were reached about noon. Hot meals were served and the men turned in to rest.	K32

WAR DIARY
or
INTELLIGENCE SUMMARY.
(Erase heading not required.)

Army Form C. 2118.

Instructions regarding War Diaries and Intelligence Summaries are contained in F. S. Regs., Part II. and the Staff Manual respectively. Title pages will be prepared in manuscript.

Place	Date	Hour	Summary of Events and Information	Remarks and references to Appendices
WIPERNINCK	1917 April 20		Instructions awaited organizing and cleaning up. Co.	App. K.33
			Warning order was received that the Division would march	" K.34
			carrying caps only. 2Lt R.N GRIFFINS and 2Lt S.WHEELS RTONS	
			W.C. DAVEY, C.WALKER, N.BAYRIGHT, F.Y. SHEPPERSON & A.WHITESIDE Officers X.95 reported	
			their arrival	
	21		In accordance with Brigade Order No.122 and 2Lt C Lowing App. K.93	
			App. K.36 the battalion moved off at 6.50 a.m. and commenced	App. K.35
			the march for TUNNELLERS Camp (Farm Shelter). This Camp was	
			reached about 10.30 a.m. but billetting was not completed	
			until 5.0 p.m. No reinforcements arrived	
			until from ? as the road to be crossed.	
TUNNELLERS CAMP Farm Shelter	22		Cleaning up baths. Welfare. No reinforcements arrived.	
	23		Training	
	24		In accordance with 86 Inf. Bde. B.M.148 "Battalion Order 2Lb4" App. K.35a. App.K.35a	
			the Battalion supplied a working party of 4 Officers and 400 O. Ranks	
			for the Construction of a line of defence in front of POPERINGHE. The	
			party moving off at 7. a.m. concentration about 5.30 p.m. &c.	

WAR DIARY
or
INTELLIGENCE SUMMARY.
(Erase heading not required.)

Army Form C. 2118.

Instructions regarding War Diaries and Intelligence Summaries are contained in F.S. Regs., Part II. and the Staff Manual respectively. Title pages will be prepared in manuscript.

Place	Date	Hour	Summary of Events and Information	Remarks and references to Appendices
HUMBERCAMP CAMP (P.25 SH27)	1916 April 24		Remainder of the Battalion (namely Scout M.G. and sanitary Sections) LieutT.C.GIBBS, R.MASON, R.H.H.SHARP, SH.BROOKS, J.S.OHAM, 2nd Lt E.C. FOX and S.O.Read rejoined. Nothing to report since arrival.	
	26		Training. At 12.50 p.m. warning orders were received that the Division would be prepared to move at short notice this order was duly issued to Companies. At 6 p.m. verbal orders from Brigade stated Battalion would prepare to move at once. At 10 p.m. Battalion orders issued with Brigade Orders No 128 attached verbal orders issued by the Brigade Major (App K 29) Moved off en-echelon with Brigade.	App K 36 App K 37 " K 39
COIGNEUX	26		Operation which were reached at 3.30 a.m. At 4 a.m. all O'Commg were called to Brigade HQ where Commander issued tomorrows Orders - Battalion would move into Kents trenches (at sq.G.H30.G.2.d) [sketch 28] This commenced at 4.45 a.m. and was completed by the Battalion and teams got under cover by 7 a.m. Orders were received that the Battalion might be called upon to occupy and organise an alternative line of defence. One E and one S of OUDENDON - these were duly reconnoitred by	App K 39

WAR DIARY
or
INTELLIGENCE SUMMARY.
(Erase heading not required.)

Army Form C. 2118.

Instructions regarding War Diaries and Intelligence Summaries are contained in F. S. Regs. Part II. and the Staff Manual respectively. Title pages will be prepared in manuscript.

Place	Date	Hour	Summary of Events and Information	Remarks and references to Appendices
OUDERDOM	1918 April 26		All concerned anticipative dispositions arranged (App K40) Officers patrols were also sent out here or four times a day daily from today. Onwards to reconnoitre the front line and out ... with the tribes in front. The high division was found to be holding the line in front.	App K40
			In many M.V. guns were active and many shell fell into battalion area. The night passed quietly. A reconnaissance of the LA CLYTTE – HALLEBAST line was carried out by an officer.	" K41
	27		party (App K42) This line was again reconnoitred by an officer and party and with periscopes at 3 p.m. (App K43) M.V guns were again active and shells fell in and around the battalion area. Companies were ordered to prepare positions in the neighbouring trenches or to dig shell slits for the men to take cover in the event of heavy shelling during night.	" K42 " K43
	28		The day passed quietly, nothing of importance to report except to usual patrols sent up to the front line. Cookers Lewis Guns and S.A.A. limbers which sent up to men have been with battalion since.	App K44

WAR DIARY
or
INTELLIGENCE SUMMARY
(Erase heading not required.)

Army Form C. 2118.

Instructions regarding War Diaries and Intelligence Summaries are contained in F. S. Regs., Part II. and the Staff Manual respectively. Title pages will be prepared in manuscript.

Place	Date	Hour	Summary of Events and Information	Remarks and references to Appendices
OUDERDOM	April 25th 1916		TUNNELLERS' Camp area returned to Transport Lines. At 9.15 a.m. orders were received hurriedly to move at an hour's notice and an Officer was despatched to await at Brigade for orders. A stragglers post was sent out by D Coy.	Appendix
		10.45 am	Soon firing on the front line area was heavy and from this had the enemy gradually put a barrage on the rear areas including the battalion positions which lasted until 11 a.m. This was heard about 7 a.m. and several direct hits on huts and on shelters were known about. My casualties being known. It was later reported that the enemy had attacked heavily along the whole Corps front but had been every where repulsed. This report at 11 p.m. area shelling the back areas heavily. About noon the Officer sent to Brigade yesterday returned with orders that no stand is to move was ordered.	

WAR DIARY
or
INTELLIGENCE SUMMARY.

(Erase heading not required.)

Army Form C. 2118.

Place	Date	Hour	Summary of Events and Information	Remarks and references to Appendices
OUDERDOM	1918 April 30		Our guns were active from about 12.30 a.m. to 1.30 a.m. and again from 2.30 a.m. to around daylight. Morning quiet.	
			Learnt that the Portugals would relieve the right sector of the 21st	App K45
			Division probably on the night 1/2 nd May.	
			4.30 p.m. Enemy shelled the battens in the vicinity of the battalion	
			very heavily and followed this by a suspected shell about	
			6.30 p.m. Capt E.J. THISGOOD, Capt A.J. GREEN, Lieuts. G.W. DAY, W. UNDERWOOD	
			and Lieut. G.E. WALTHO and 18 o. Ranks reinforcements reported	
			their arrival.	

J.O. Rudsdell, Major
Commanding 9th Hertfordshire Regt.

Copy No 6.   6th Bn. Cheshire Regiment Order No. 5   21-4-16

1.   MOVE. The Battalion less Transport will move by march route to CAMP DE CAMP, WOLVERGHEM, (T.S.central, Sheet 28) tomorrow.

2.   PARADE. The Battalion will parade on the field adjoining the O.R.Stores at 3.45 p.m.

3.   Company stores and blankets (rolled in bundles of ten) will be stacked at company offices ready to load on limbers. at 2 p.m.

    Transport Officer will arrange transport to move these to CAMP DE CAMP before 4 p.m. and hand them over to the billeting party.

4.   Quartermaster Stores will move to the Transport Lines, the move to be completed by 4.p.m.

5.   Billeting party of 1 N.C.O. per company and H.Q. will parade at D.Coy H.Q. at 8.30 a.m. under 2nd Lieut. A.E.Dashboard. This party will report at the new camp at R.E.Q.

Copy No.   1 C.O.   Captain,
           2 Adjt.   Adjutant, 6th Bn. Cheshire Regiment.
           3 A Coy
           4 B "
           5 C "
           6 D "
           7 H.Q.
           8
           9
          10 R.S.M.
          11 M.O.
          12 File

To Headquarters C.O/15
5th Bde

Battalion arrived in GABLE CAMP 5.15 pm. Casualties NIL.

1/4/18

L/Col
Comdg 7th Battn

A 22/308.

URGENT.

All Coys & HQ.

Refer Bn Order No 6 para 3 —
the battn will parade as detailed
at the road junction T.5.c.65.95
ready to move off at 2.30 pm
Please initial & return to bearer

12.25 pm
7/4/18.
A
B
C
D
HQ

D. Greville Capt.
ADJUTANT.
9th (SERVICE) Bn. CHESHIRE REGT.

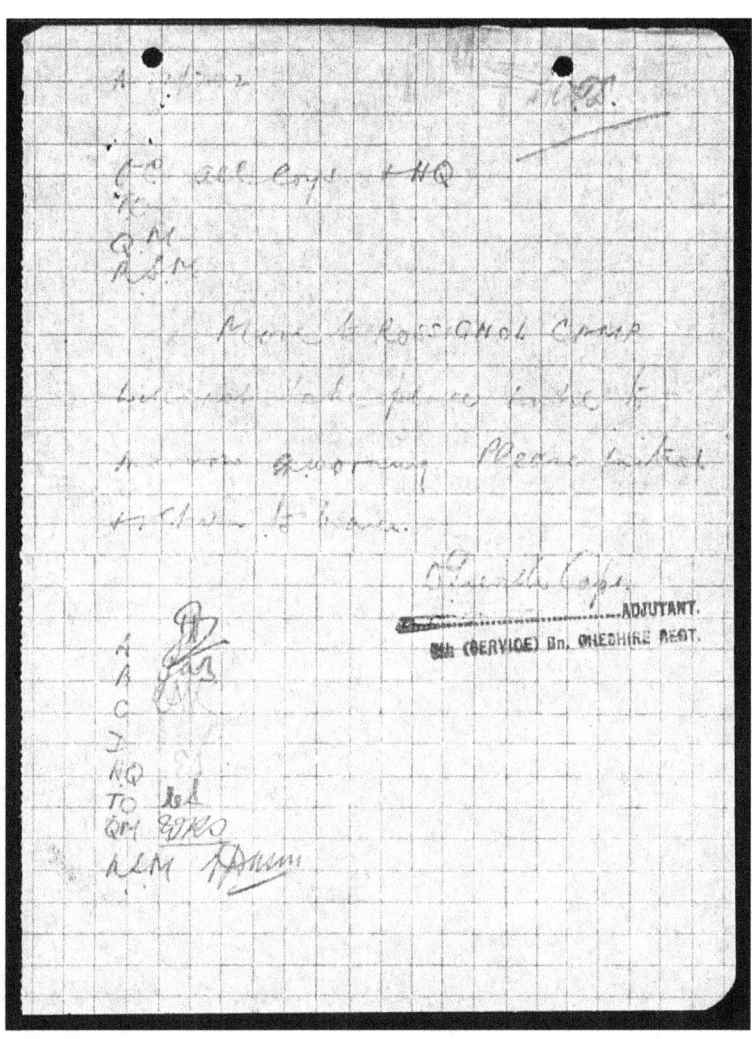

From LASSOO.   (Sgd) B.im THURN, Capt.
12.10 p.m.   Bde. Major.

Copy of Wire to 1/4th K.S.L.I.

        B.A.130   10th.

        You will move on to HILL 63 at once and occupy the high ground
AAA Enemy are reportedto be in PLOEGSTEERT VILLAGE AAA Situation in
MESSINES is obscure AAA You will establish a report centre at Road
Junction T.18.a.45.75 AAA Brigade H.Q. are proceeding temporarily
to H.Q. 25th Divn. RAVELSBERG S.16.d. AAA Bde. Advanced Report
Centre will be established at LA TROMPE CABARET T.9.d.3.1. AAA 1st
Line Transport lews Lewis Guns and drums will proceed to T.8.d.3.2.
AAA Report the position you occupy to Adv. Bde. H.Q.

From 56th Bde.   (sgd) B.im THURN, Capt.
Time 9.45 a.m.   Bde. Major.
                        -------------------- -------

                        SECRET.

Copy of Wire to 56th T.M.Bty.

        B.A.131.   10th.

        Enemy are reported to be in PLOEGSTEERT VILLAGE AAA Situation
in MESSINES is obscure AAA You will move your Battery to Adv. Bde.
H.Q. which is being established at Cross Roads T.9.d.3.1.

From 56th Bde.   (Sgd) B.im THURN, Capt.
                                                Bde. Major.

Copy of Wire to 1/4 K.S.L.I.

    B.A.135.   10th.

You are ordered to hold GAS Trench which runs N. and S. just West of U.13. central AAA Also a trench parrallel to and about 300^x East of GAS TRENCH AAA You must deny this high ground to the enemy AAA You must pay particular attention to both your flanks as enemy are reported to be in PLOEGSTEERT WOOD and in low ground to your NORTH AAA 25th Div. intend to establish a line facing Eastwards between PLOEGSTEERT VILLAGE and the river to the South of the Village AAA Various Bns. of 25th Division are said to be holding ridge some 2,000^x to the East of GAS Tr. but parties of the enemy are said to be both to the N. and S. of them AAA Bde. H.Q. will be at T.20.a.6.4. AAA Adv. Bde. H.Q. at LEEUNER FARM T.10.d.4.3. AAA Please report disposition as soon as possible.

From 56th Bde.   (Sgd) B.im THURN, Capt.
Time 1.0 p.m.   Bde. Major.

Copy of Wire to 10 Worc. 1/4 K.S.L.I. 10 R.War. R. 8 Glouc.
                9 Ches. R.   19th Div. G. 8 N.Staff. R. and
                O.C. KEMMEL DEFENCES.

B.M.X.104.   16th.

The KEMMEL - VIERSTRAAT Defences will be manned as follows:-
1. 10/Worc. R. on left of 8 N.Staff.R. from N.27.b.5.8. to LA POLKA N.22.c.2.8. AAA 8 Glouc. R. on left of 9 Ches. R. from N.20.d.8.0. to N.15.c.2.0.

2. 1/4 K.S.L.I. will take up a position in reserve in N.20.a. & b.

3. Moves will be undertaken forthwith.

4. Dispositions will be in depth.

5. Units concerned will report by runner their arrival in new position and location of their Battn. H.Q. as soon as possible to Bde. H.Q. AAA Acknowledge.

                                        (Sd) W.S.SCAMMELL, Capt.
From 57th Inf. Bde.   B.M. 57th Bde.

SECRET.

                 9 Cheshire,
Copy of Wire to 1/4 K.S.L.I. 8 N.Staff. R. 56th T.M.B.
               19th Divn. 57th Bde. 58th Bde.

    BA. 193.   16th.

1.   The Bde. will operate under the orders of 56th Bde. H.Qrs.

2.   (a) There is at present no prospect of relief and men should not be allowed to buoy themselves up with rumours of large numbers of French Troops coming to their assistance.

      (b) We have to fight it out where we are unless orders to withdraw are issued from the Div., and it is up to us to prove after all these days of fighting whether we or the Germans can stick it longest.

      (c) It is anticipated that the enemy will attack KEMMEL HILL.

3.   (a) 9th Cheshire and 8 N.Staffords are already in position for the defence of the KEMMEL HILL.

      (b) 1. 1/4 K.S.L.I. will be in Bde. Reserve and will occupy the two Northern Spurs of the HILL in squares N.20. a and b., facing roughly S.E. and keeping to W. of KEMMEL - LA CLYTTE Road.
         ii. The Bn. must be prepared either to hold their ground or to cover the withdrawal of the remainder of the Bde. in case of necessity, or to counterattack under orders from the Bde.

4.   The left boundary of the Div. runs (backward) from LA POLKA N.22.c. - POMPIER ESTAMINET N.14.a.5.0 passing just N.E. of SCHERPENBERG Hill M.10.central.
    The right boundary - from Western slopes of KEMMEL HILL to WESTOUTRE.

5.   Any change in dispositions, such as a swinging back of the line, which may occur on the left flank of the Bde. does not mean that there should be any corresponding change in the dispositions of the Bde.

6.   Reports. -
        (a) Bns. will keep Bde. informed of any change of position of their Bn. H.Qrs.
        (b) Bde. Adv. Report Centre - dugout 150^x S. of BUTTERFLY FM.
        (c) Bde. H.Q. - SCHERPENBERG HILL.
Bns. will endeavour to establish visual communication with Bde. H.Q. at 4. p.m.

7.   ACKNOWLEDGE.

                                   (Sgd) B.im THURN, Capt.
                                        Brigade Major.
56th Bde.
2.0 p.m.

SECRET.

Copy of Wire to 9/Cheshires, 1/4th Shrops. L.I., 8/N.Staff. R.
    56th T.M.Bty, B.T.O.

   B.A.215   17th.

                WARNING ORDER.

1.   19th Division will be relieved by the 28th French Div. on night 18/19th April.

2.   French troops who will occupy KEMMEL Defences will be there in position by noon 18th April, but British troops now occupying MONT KEMMEL will not be withdrawn before 8.30 p.m. 18th - responsibility for the defence of the HILL however, passes to the French at noon.

3.   (a) French dispositions have not been notified, but Bn. Commanders should endeavour to get into touch with any Bn. Commanders of the French Army who may happen to be in their areas and obtain from them the French dispositions,
     (b) Should it be found that any of the French Troops are located in front of our outposts the outposts must be particularly cautioned of the fact.

4.   Although the French are responsible after noon April 18th Bn. Commanders will continue after that hour to take all the usual precautions for the defence of their line.

From 56th Bde.   (Sgd) B.im THURN, Capt.
Time 11 p.m.   Brigade Major.

56th Infantry Brigade S.C./1.

9/Ches. R.   19th Divn.
1/4 Shrops. L.I.   57th Inf. Bde.
8/N.Staff. R.   56th Inf. Bde.
56th T.M.Bty.

    Reference B.A.229 - on relief units will move to areas in Square L.34.

    (1) Route. CANADA CORNER - WESTOUTRE - thence POPERINGHE Road to G.32.d.3.2. - towards Cross Roads L.34.d.0.4.

    (2) Control Posts. will be established as under:-

        (a) CANADA CORNER.
        (b) WESTOUTRE (M.9.c.5.3.)
        (c) G.32.d.8.2.

    (3) Guides. Arrangements will be made by Staff Captain for Battalion Guides to be at Road Junction L.35.c. to guide units to destination.

    (4) Food. will be ready on arrival.

    (5) Lewis Gun limbers and 5 limbers per battalion for sick will meet units half way between CANADA CORNER and WESTOUTRE.

                              (Sgd) B. im THURN. Capt.
                                    Brigade Major,
18th April 1918.   56th Infantry Brigade.

A 22/293   W.D

WARNING ORDER.

O.C Coys & HQ. R.S.M

1. The Brigade moves into camps about F.27.a tomorrow, 21st instant.

2. A billeting party composed as follows will assemble at the Company's billet at 5.45 am:—
   Lieut. C.H. JONES
   1 NCO per each coy and HQ.
   the latter must be in possession of their Coy's requirements.

3. O.C 'C' Coy will detail a party of 1 officer and 100 O.R. to proceed as advance party to pitch tents. This party is to report to the Staff Captain at roads junction in F 21.c at 7-15 am, together with the above billeting party, and will parade at 5.45 am under O.C 'C' Coy's arrangements.

4. Dress — for all ranks — fighting order.

5. Officers kits, Blankets, kits and all stores must be ready for loading at 5.30 am — dumped near the entrance to the billet occupied by

companies. Each coy. will detail 1 NCO
being Gunner to accompany the M.G. limbers.
6. Reveille 4.30 am
   Breakfast 5 am
   Sick parade – after arrival in new
   area.
   Parade: Coys will parade on Coy. parade grounds
   ready to move off at 6.30am.
7 Please initial and return to
   bearer

                            D Lewelle Capt & Adjt.
        (Sd) 6th CHESHIRE Regt.

11.5 pm
20/4/18

A ack/
B C.R.R. 11.20 P.M
C /M/
D /T/ 12.15.
HQ
RSM

After orders
           RSM will arrange loading
party – blankets to be in bundles of 10
        B Maps.

S.P. : N.

To O.C.   Company,

Reference Map Sheet 27 and 28
----

1. The Brigade has been made responsible for the construction of a line of defence from G.15.a.70.75 (POPERINGHE - BUSSEBOOM Road) exclusive) to G.9.d.50.65. The line will be continued North by the 5th S.W.B. 81st Field Coy R.E. will work in co-operation with the Brigade.

2. Work on this line will be carried out by the Battalion on the following dates:-

   April 24th, 27th, 30th, May 3rd, and so on.

3. The following principles will be observed in construction of the defences:-

   (a) A continuous trench line with one or more barbed wire Apron fences will be constructed in the first instance. This will be strengthened later by the construction of support and reserve systems and tactical points.
   (b) The first continuous trench must have good observation and field of fire to the front wherever possible. It should not be sited further forward as a general rule than 200 yards from the tactical crest line.
   (c) One strong tactical point to be held by one battalion and 8 machine guns will be organised about G.9.c. and d. (covering BUSSEBOOM Road).
   (d) Trenches will as far as possible be sited so that they can be drained in to the existing land drainage system. The drains composing this system should be cleared out before or concurrently with the excavation of the trenches which will drain into them.
   (e) Trenches will be dug as deep as the state of the ground permits. It should be possible almost everywhere with careful drainage to make them of the section given below so that they can take a small FRAME. A frame.

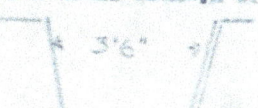

   (f) All earth excavated should be thrown up on the parapet side of the trench leaving a 2-ft. berm from the edge. The parapet and parados will be completed by earth from borrow pits to the section shown below:-

   The borrow pits must in no case be nearer than 20 feet to the trench.

4. (a) Hours of work will be:-
      9.30 a.m. to 12.30 p.m.
      Dinners
      and 2.p.m. to 4.p.m.

   (b) Companies will march to G.9.c.30.15 to be there by 9.30 a.m. At this point there is a notice board "PENGUIN CAMP" and Os. C.Coy's will be met by representative of 81st Field Coy R.E. who will guide to site of Coy's task and generally supervise.

--2--

5. Route to be followed:-

   (a) **Infantry** - Road junction L.4.b.9.1 - track junction
   L.11.a.3.9. Road junction L.12.c.10.45 - Road junction
   L.12.c.70.82 - thence through railway siding - G.8.c.2.4 -
   thence path to G.8.c.8.6. thence cart track to G.8.d.8.6.

   (b) **Transport** - through POPERINGHE.

   Intervals of 100 yards will be maintained between Companies
   on line of march.

6. A.C. and D.Coys will compose the working party for tomorrow
   and will work on the line from left to right in the order
   A. C. D.
   The following will not be taken on parade but will attend
   their classes as for today:-

   Scouts attending Bde Class.
   Lewis Gunners " "   "
   "   "   " Battn Class.

   Other men necessary for duties inside the Company may be left
   off the parade at the descretion of the O.C. Coy, but the
   minimum number of O.R. to be on parade and actually available
   for digging (i.e. exclusive of Sergeants and above who do
   not dig) must be 175 O.R. All officers will parade.

7. Dress:- Fighting Order.

8. **Parade** A.C. and D Coys will parade ready to move off at
   7.a.m. in that order. Tools will be drawn from transport
   on arrival at G.9.c.30.15. and must be loaded on to limbers
   again on completion of day's work.
   Transport Officer will arrange to have cookers at
   track junction G.9.c.30.15. by 12.30.p.m. and tool limbers
   there by 8.30 a.m. and collect the latter again at 4.p.m.

9. Teas will be served on return to camp about 5.30 p.m.

                                              Captain,
                              Adjutant, 9th Bn.Cheshire Regiment.

23rd April 1918.

WAR DIARY
or
INTELLIGENCE SUMMARY.
(Erase heading not required.)

Army Form C. 2118.

9th Cheshire Regt

Vol 32

Place	Date	Hour	Summary of Events and Information	Remarks and references to Appendices
OUDERDOM (G 24 Sheet 28)	1918 May 1		The day was moderately quiet. A warning order was received that K Brigade would relieve a Brigade of the 9th Division on the line in front of DICKEBUSCH lake on the night 1st/2nd May. Companies were duly warned. (App.K16) In accordance with BrigBS orver attached A2 (App.K17) rations were received about 1 P.M. and moved's Companies come the Battalion moved off at 8.20 p.m. march Q at G 24 Central (Sheet 28) by Companies at 10.00 P.M. advance commenced 6 H 23 a 01 and to DICKEBUSCH BERK. There guides from the 17th and 10th Liverpool's met the Regt met Companies and guided them into the trenches. On completion of relief the dispositions of the Battalion were front line from H 3b c 63 b H 36 8.2 m sub A Coy Centre C Coy left. B Coy and B Coy in reserve in front of SCOTTISHWOOD Bat Coy. HQ Coy to take over at 11.30 and 1. 20 am Battalion was on the left. Battalion being wtouch with the 6th Wares of the 5th Inf Brigade on the left and to 14 K.S.L.I of the Brigade in reserve on the right. Lieut F.E. EVANS reported arrival.	App K16 K17 32 E. 137 Ment

WAR DIARY
or
INTELLIGENCE SUMMARY.
(Erase heading not required.)

Army Form C. 2118.

Place	Date	Hour	Summary of Events and Information	Remarks and references to Appendices
DICKEBUSCH HUTS	1918 May 2		The relief was completed about 1.30 a.m. although not reported until later on account of one Company report being delayed. Patrols were sent out but there was no sign of any enemy Concentration. Also warnings were received (App K&Q) of possible enemy attacks. No warning shots were duly passed on to Companies. There was however no violent action by the enemy at dawn - the forward area and the reserve line SCOTTISH WOOD were shelled and desultory Shelling continued throughout the day. Rations and water were brought up to Bath. HQ and distributed to Companies about 10.30 p.m. Positions for supporting platoons of front line Companies were selected and work commenced. Quiet night.	App K&Q , K&Q
	3		Artilleries of both sides were active at dawn. A forward Scottn. HQ. was established about H.35.b central. At 10 a.m however the enemy started a heavy bombardment of SCOTTISH WOOD and the Camp on the Nicolson Ridge of the wood. Unfortunately a direct hit on the HQ. post was obtained and	

WAR DIARY or INTELLIGENCE SUMMARY.

Army Form C. 2118.

Place	Date	Hour	Summary of Events and Information	Remarks and references to Appendices
DICKEBUSCH LAKE	1915 May 3		Several casualties caused. The Reserve Company was also heavily shelled but were now formed up. The afternoon passed fairly quietly, but guns were again active in the evening against the Companies' areas. Rations were again brought up safely. C Company 2nd Batt. H.Q. moved into a dugout at H.32 & 36, leaving a rear party at the lakeside. The night passed quietly. A warning was received that an enemy attack was expected. Companies were warned but no attack took place. Patrols were out and beyond heavy slight movement, there was no sign of the enemy's presence and no indications of any concentration (App. K.51). One Company of the GLOUCESTER Regt. took up positions in the "Reserve line and was to hold it with Reserve Company Counter-attacking. There was no	App.K.50 App.K.51
	4		Normal shelling during the day on the Reserve line and SCOTTISH WOOD, the latter place being heavily shelled. Warning Order (App.K.53) was received that the 98th Brigade would relieve	App.K.52 K.53

WAR DIARY
INTELLIGENCE SUMMARY
(Erase heading not required.)

Army Form C. 2118.

Place	Date	Hour	Summary of Events and Information	Remarks and references to Appendices
LOCKREBUSCHEN LAKE	1918 May 4		The Brigade that night Advance parties arrived about 8 p.m. and the relief was completed (according to BRIG 114 and Battn. Order No 10 App K 54) by 2 am (App K 55). The Battalion marched to billets in huts at	App K 54 " K 55
	5		G.16.6.4.8 which were reached about 4.30 a.m (App K 56) about 7.30 a.m a message was received from Brigade (App K 57) Conveying the warning order contained in SC 199 - App K 54) that the Brigade would move to B.8 area (Sheet 27) today. Later however, about 12 noon orders were received that this move would take place (App K 58) and at 4.45 p.m the Battalion moved off - 100 yards	" K 56 " K 57 App K 58
A.8.C.3.b (Sheet 27)			distance between Companies - and marched to field at A.8.C.3.b (Sheet 27) where a camp was being erected by the Engineers. Unfortunately, before this was completed a heavy Thunder Storm came on and the men were drenched before Bivouacs were erected. The move was completed by 5 p.m.	App K 59
	6		The morning was very wet and it was difficult to keep the men dry. Scotch broth at Tamosh for all in the afternoon the	

WAR DIARY
or
INTELLIGENCE SUMMARY.
(Erase heading not required.)

Army Form C. 2118.

Instructions regarding War Diaries and Intelligence Summaries are contained in F. S. Regs., Part II. and the Staff Manual respectively. Title pages will be prepared in manuscript.

Place	Date	Hour	Summary of Events and Information	Remarks and references to Appendices
I.8.c.3.6. (Sheet 27)	1916 May 6		Brigade was ordered in Divisional Reserve and all units were under half an hours notice to move. (App K.60)	App K.60
	7		Relieving up and refitting. Warning order received that the Brigade would relieve the 58th Inf. Brigade on the night of 9/10 May	"K.61
	8		At 7.45 a.m. a stand to was ordered (App K.62) Heavy gun fire was heard up on the front line and it was afterwards ascertained that the enemy had attacked to the right of the Divisional front in the neighbourhood of RIDGE WOOD and to the right. This stand to was cancelled at 9.30 a.m. Capt. S.R. ALEXANDER and Lieuts. B. BERRY and F.W. JONES reported arrival.	"K.62 "K.63
	9		Machine Gun was received that the Brigade will not relieve the 58th Inf. Bde on the night 10th/11th May	"K.64
	10		Advance parties proceeded at 5.10 p.m. to reconnoitre the new front the Battalion moved off at 9.45 a.m. carrying two days rations entrained at FOUR WIND (5.17 d Sheet 27) and carried out the relief of the 6th WILTS as detailed in 58th Inf. Bde Order No. 125 and Bn Order No. 9 (App K.65) The Surplus personnel	"K.65

WAR DIARY
INTELLIGENCE SUMMARY

(Erase heading not required.)

Army Form C. 2118.

Place	Date	Hour	Summary of Events and Information	Remarks and references to Appendices
26 c 3 6 Sheet 57	1918 May 10		Personnel (6 offs. 130 O.R.) proceeded to the transport lines. It was understood that the Brigade would be relieved on this night.	
	11		12/13th May (App 6). Owing to every shelling the detraining point ("PIONIER") could not be reached in train and the Battalion detrained 700 yards short of this point. The movement was also being shelled and the relief was therefore somewhat delayed. It was completed however by 2.30 a.m. (App. K 65 (6)). The Battalion's dispositions were on the 9/10 & 11th from 1.30 c 4.5 to 14.30 4.4.6 – three Coys holding these positions – distributed in depths as follows, right Coy. centre B Coy, left D Coy – C Coy being in Batt. reserve in H 23 c Battalion HQ was situated at H 23 a 9 7. The remainder of the night was quietly spent. On the Next night work was carried out on the H.Q. 2 line by the 3 Coys holding it (App K 67).	App x 5 6 App x 65 (6) " K 67
	12		About 2.a.m. the French 60th Inf Regt. took over the sector on the Brigade's right and the liaison arrangements detailed in	" K 67

WAR DIARY
or
INTELLIGENCE SUMMARY.
(Erase heading not required.)

Army Form C. 2118.

Instructions regarding War Diaries and Intelligence Summaries are contained in F. S. Regs., Part II. and the Staff Manual respectively. Title pages will be prepared in manuscript.

Place	Date	Hour	Summary of Events and Information	Remarks and references to Appendices
H.23.d.7.7.	1918 May 12		B.M. 100-162 and Batten A.2.137/11 (all App K.68) were carried out.	App K68
			Warnings were received and passed on to Companies of an expected German attack (App K69). The morning however passed	"K69
			normally. our artillery carrying out Counter-preparations on the enemy lines. The orders for the relief by the 1/4 LEICESTERS	
			were received (App K.70 (a)) and in accordance with these additional orders	"K70
			No16 (App K.70 b) the Battalion duly handed over the relief	
	13		was carried out without hindrance and completed by 12.30 a.m. (App K70c) and the Battalion proceeded by light railway	
L.8.C.36			and route march to Camp at L.8.C.36. When it reached	"K.71
		2.45 a.m	at 2.45 a.m (App K.71) the camp. The Surplus personnel were already accommodated. Breakfasts were served to the men	
			on arrival and the morning was spent in rest. The day turned out very wet. 2nd Lts L.COOPER, J.H.SWIFT and	
			62 O.R reinforcements reported arrival	

WAR DIARY
INTELLIGENCE SUMMARY.
(Erase heading not required.)

Army Form C. 2118.

Place	Date	Hour	Summary of Events and Information	Remarks and references to Appendices
H.23.a.77 (Sheet 27)	1918 May 14		Rest, cleaning up and inspections. The first orders for a divisional move by rail were received (App K71(a)) and the necessary warning orders were issued to Companies (App K71(c)). Enemy aircraft dropped bombs in the vicinity of ST JAN-TER-BIEZEN during the night (which was bright moonlight until midnight)	App K71(a) " (c)
	15		Training. Further details and definite orders for the move were received (App K71(b)) and orders for the Battalion move were issued to all concerned in Bn Order No 11. (App K71.d) The enemy's high velocity guns were active during the day and 1 man was wounded on a company parade by shrapnel. Enemy planes were again active at night. Majors G.MARTIN assumed States Command of Battalion.	" (b) " (d)
	16		"B" Coy and advance parties moved off at 10 a.m and duly entrained in accordance with Bn Order No 11. (App K71(e)) All tents, bivouacs, etc. were struck by 10.30 a.m and handed over to a representative of the 33rd Division. The Battalion duly moved off	" (e)

Army Form C. 2118.

WAR DIARY
or
INTELLIGENCE SUMMARY.
(Erase heading not required.)

Instructions regarding War Diaries and Intelligence Summaries are contained in F. S. Regs., Part II. and the Staff Manual respectively. Title pages will be prepared in manuscript.

Place	Date	Hour	Summary of Events and Information	Remarks and references to Appendices
	May 1918 16		at 2 p.m. arr. entrained at WAAYENBURG, so outside an for Order No. 11.	App K71(A)
			This was completed by 7.20 p.m. D'tory also carried out their entrainment without incident. All trains moved off punctually	
			The route was via BOULOGNE - ABBEVILLE - NOYELLES - PONTOISE -	
	17		outskirts of PARIS - CHATEAU THIERRY - CHALONS.	
	18		VITRY-LA-VILLE the detraining station was reached at 10.30 a.m. Here the Battalion was met by the Staff Captain who directed the	
LA CHAUSSÉE			way to LA CHAUSSÉE, where the Battalion's billets were situated. This involved a march of about 6 kilos which proved very trying owing to the great heat of the day. Billets were reached	
			by 9.15 p.m. (App K72). All companies were very comfortable, the billets being exceedingly good. The surrounding country although not offering the best facilities for training was very fine and the Canal afforded good bathing which was much enjoyed by all ranks during the hot weather that followed	App K72

WAR DIARY
or
INTELLIGENCE SUMMARY.

(Erase heading not required.)

Army Form C. 2118.

Place	Date	Hour	Summary of Events and Information	Remarks and references to Appendices
LACHAUSSEE	1918 May 18		Rest and cleaning up.	
	19		Church Parade and inspections	
	20		Training. All Battalion Commanders met the Corps Commander	App. K73
			at Brigade H.Q. at 9.45 a.m.	
	21		Training.	
	22		It was decided to take greater advantage of the early hours of	
			the morning and avoid training before the hottest part of the	
			day. Consequently from today onwards first parade was at	
			4.30 a.m.	
	23		Training.	
	24		Training. The Corps Commander Lieut. Gen. Sir Ivylmer Hunter-Weston	
			delivered a lecture to all officers and N.C.O's	
			of the Division at Divisional H.Q. at ST GERMAIN.	
	25		Training.	
	26		Colonel's parade and inspection. Major W.W.S. CUNNINGHAME arrived	
			to take command of the Battalion. Major J.G. MARTIN M.C. left to rejoin	
			8th N. Staff. Regt.	

WAR DIARY
or
INTELLIGENCE SUMMARY.
(Erase heading not required.)

Place	Date	Hour	Summary of Events and Information	Remarks and references to Appendices
LACHAUSSEE	1918 Nov 2nd		Evening Warning orders were received that transport must be prepared to move at short notice at an early hour on the 25th	App. K74
		6.30 a.m	Orders were received for the Transport to move to an area near TOURS. In accordance with these orders 26th Inf. Bgde B.R. 43/3 - and Bde Order No 126) the transport moved off	" K75
				" K76
		10.15 a.m	Orders were received during the morning to the effect that the Battalion itself would move by bus at night to a new area. Training was cancelled and preparations for the move made. At 8 p.m further orders were received (App. K77) and the Battalion prepared for immediate entrusing in accordance with these orders. The French lorries arrived at 11 p.m and the Battalion commenced to entrus. Embussing was completed by about midnight and the lorries moved off. Suitable personnel to the number of 4 Officers and 169 O.R. were left behind under the Command of Capt. A.J. GATCHEL, and the following were the Officers of the	" K77

WAR DIARY
or
INTELLIGENCE SUMMARY.
(Erase heading not required.)

Army Form C. 2118.

Instructions regarding War Diaries and Intelligence Summaries are contained in F. S. Regs., Part II. and the Staff Manual respectively. Title pages will be prepared in manuscript.

Place	Date	Hour	Summary of Events and Information	Remarks and references to Appendices
	Nov 1918			
	28		Fighting personnel. Major W.W.S. Cunliffe Home, Commanding Officer	
			Captain R.H.Griffiths Second in Command, Captain D. Greville Peynton	
			Capt. E.F. Thurgood OC "A" Coy. Capt S.A. Alexander OC "D" Coy. Lieut S.R. Broom,	
			OC "B" Coy. Lieut G.W. Day OC "C" Coy. Lieut T.C. Gibbs Intelligence Officer	
			Lieut F. Simcock Signalling Officer, Lieuts E.B. Evans, F.N. Jones	
			W.W. Underwood, Inglefield J.H. Swift, L. Cooper, E.C. Fox, F.V. Shipman, H.B. Wright	
			A.T. Giles, C. Walker, A.B. Inchboard, W.A.C. Doyen. Total 21	
			Officers 5.50 O.Ranks.	
	29		After an all night journey the Battalion debused about	
			1 mile North of CHAUMUZY on the CHAUMUZY - CHAMBRECY Road	
			reference map SOISSONS "100,000" about 9 a.m and verbal	
			orders were issued by the Brigade for the Battalion to	
			bivouac on the southern slopes of the high ground immediately	
			N. of CHAMBRECY. This was carried out by 11.30 a.m. (App K-18)	App K-18
			Orders confirming this were received from Brigade about half	
			an hour later and dispositions made in accordance	

WAR DIARY
INTELLIGENCE SUMMARY.
(Erase heading not required.)

Army Form C. 2118.

Place	Date	Hour	Summary of Events and Information	Remarks and references to Appendices
	1916 Nov 29		with further details (App K'g) Coy officers obtaining patrols was put out on the high ground North of VILLE-EN-TARDENOIS	App K79
SARCY			(App K80). The Brigade was later ordered to occupy the valley just West of SARCY and the Battalion move at 4.45 p.m. and took up a position in accordance with 58 Brigade B.M. 1699 (App K81). The Battalion was placed under the orders of the 58th Infantry Brigade (App K82). Orders were issued to the Commanding Officers to move the Battalion on the early morning to the vicinity of SARCY village and to establish H.Q. and the	App K81 " K82
	30		village. This was carried out starting at 4.30 a.m. as detailed in App K83. Reconnaissances were carried out of the ridge just N.W. of SARCY with a view to holding it. At 11.45 a.m. orders were received to take up these positions to allow other units of the 58th Brigade to withdraw through this line and to gain touch on the right with the 56th Brigade whose left was to swing back to SARCY village (App K84). This was	(App K83)

WAR DIARY
or
INTELLIGENCE SUMMARY.
(Erase heading not required.)

Army Form C. 2118.

Place	Date	Hour	Summary of Events and Information	Remarks and references to Appendices
SARCY	19/6 May 30		Completed by 1 p.m. There were no troops by this time on the left and no enemy scouts could be observed in BOIS D'AULNAY. The left Company "A" Coy formed a defensive flank running towards the farm 1 Kilometre S.E. of the Bois D'AULNAY (reference Map appx 65 SOISSONS 1/100,000) "B" Coy also sent a platoon to reinforce this defensive flank. In a short time onwards considerable enemy movement was seen both of scouts and of larger bodies who followed them up. The enemy shelling also increased and by evening was fairly heavy, especially on SARCY village. The enemy attempted to advance from the BOIS D'AULNAY but was held up by the fire of our Lewis Gund and rifles on the left. Owing to the situation on the left a withdrawal of the Division to a line just South of SARCY village was ordered at 7.30 p.m. and the Battalion with drew by Companies from the left, starting at 8.30 p.m. This was most successfully carried out without casualties	

WAR DIARY
or
INTELLIGENCE SUMMARY.
(Erase heading not required.)

Army Form C. 2118.

Place	Date	Hour	Summary of Events and Information	Remarks and references to Appendices
SARCY	1918 May 30		and without attracting the attention of the enemy. The only casualties sustained up to the present were, Officers: Lieut R.S. EVANS and Lt. L. COOPER 2nd Lt ABINGHBOARD all wounded and 22 other Ranks. By midnight fresh positions had been taken up astride the CHAMBRECY - SARCY road cover on the high ground	
SOUTH of SARCY	31		1 mile North of CHAMBRECY and also that ½ mile South of SARCY. The night passed extremely quietly. The Transport which had arrived at LA NEUVILLE during the day brought rations up to Battalion HQ (in the small wood ½ mile N of the B in CHAMBRECY). The morning passed quietly and certain minor readjustments of the Battalion line were made by the Commanding Officer. Considerable enemy movement was seen however both North of SARCY Church, in the vicinity of BOIS D'AULNAY. Small former bodies were seen giving the impression that the enemy was massing and an attack was expected. (The Tahobot moved	

Army Form C. 2118.

WAR DIARY
or
INTELLIGENCE SUMMARY.
(Erase heading not required.)

Instructions regarding War Diaries and Intelligence Summaries are contained in F. S. Regs., Pwt. II. and the Staff Manual respectively. Title pages will be prepared in manuscript.

Place	Date	Hour	Summary of Events and Information	Remarks and references to Appendices
SOUTH of SARCY.	19th May 21		to South of NANTEUIL) Enemy M.G's were fairly active on the front line during the latter end of the morning and about 12.30 p.m. the enemy commenced heavy shelling which increased in violence on the whole of the Battalion front, and on the left. Many casualties were sustained during this shelling as the Companies were lying out in the open with practically no cover. At 5 p.m. enemy troops were seen advancing in attack formation to the WEST of the CHAMBRECY – SARCY road and the shelling and Machine Gun fire especially on the valley due South of SARCY became very heavy. Troops on the left of the Battalion caused the Battalion's left were driven back of the high ground and CHAMBRECY Village was in danger of falling into the hands of the enemy who were now attacking in great numbers. The Commanding Officer, Major Cunninghame however riding out on his horse, rallied the left and taking the other	APPX K

WAR DIARY
or
INTELLIGENCE SUMMARY.
(Erase heading not required.)

Army Form C. 2118.

Instructions regarding War Diaries and Intelligence Summaries are contained in F. S. Regs., Part II. and the Staff Manual respectively. Title pages will be prepared in manuscript.

Place	Date	Hour	Summary of Events and Information	Remarks and references to Appendices
SOUTH D-SARCY	1915 Nov 3		Two Companies this assistance counter attacked the enemy on the high ground N of CIMIÈRES. This Counter-attack had to advance through heavy enemy Machine Gun and Artillery fire and the Commanding Officer's horse was shot under him. He carried on on foot however, and led the Battalion right up to the top where they delivered their assault and completely regained the old position. The enemy however, who had strong reserves, came again attacked and succeeded in dislodging the Battalion again only to be himself once more ejected by a successful Counter-attack. The 2nd Wilts Regt had been ordered to come up to reinforce and they arrived about 11 pm and, together with the Battalion, delivered a series of Counter-attacks which restored the situation so far as holding our old positions on the plateau. The enemy though still retained a footing on the Northern edge of	

WAR DIARY
OF
INTELLIGENCE SUMMARY.
(Erase heading not required.)

Army Form C. 2118.

Place	Date	Hour	Summary of Events and Information	Remarks and references to Appendices
	May 31		The platoon & Commanding Officer were wounded just before the arrival of the Mills and Lewis Cartbelliads withdrew. Capt A.H. GRIFFITHS thereupon took over the Command of the B. battalion. The casualties sustained by the Battalion in this battle were heavy. The following being Officer Casualties. Capt E.F. THURGOOD, 2nd Lt. J.H. SWIFT Killed in Action. Major W.W.S. CUNINGHAME, Capt S.A. ALEXANDER, Lieut. S. R. BROOME, F.W. JONES, N.W. UNDERWOOD, 2nd Lieuts. E.C. FOX, E.N. SHIPMAN, A.J. GIBBS, C. WALKER, W.A.C. DAVEY wounded in Action. Lieuts. T.C. GIBBS and G.W. DAY missing in action. Total 14. Other Ranks Casualties were 69 killed, wounded and missing. The night passed quietly and many wounded were brought in. The Battalion dispositions were also reorganised.	"Westminsterques" Lt. Col. O/C (3) Battn (London Regt)

Army Form C. 2118.

9th Bn
The Cheshire Rgt

WAR DIARY
or
INTELLIGENCE SUMMARY.
(Erase heading not required.)

Place	Date	Hour	Summary of Events and Information	Remarks and references to Appendices
Near CHAMBRECY	1918 June 1		The strength of the Battalion was now 4 Officers 200 Other Ranks. Officers Capt R.H.GRIFFITHS (Comdg) Capt Rev D.GREVILLE Lieut E.SIMCOCK and Lieut H.BURIGHT. The line held was facing North in front of the MONTAGNE de BLIGNY and across the valley to the stream running from the village of CHAMBRECY to SPRCY the railway bridge being in the front line. Brigade dispositions were as shown in [Bn.] 151/5 (app K88). Battalion H.Q. was established at the kink in the road 500 yards North of the R. in CHAMBRECY. by Map.	App K88
			SOISSONS 1/100,000. The transport moved to the neighbourhood of NAUTVILLERS. Except for intermittent shelling the day passed quietly. Considerable enemy movement was observed in the neighbourhood of BOIS D'AULNAY and transport and guns could be seen moving forward from LHÉRY. At 7.15 p.m. however, orders were received by the Brigade to withdraw slightly to conform with the situation on the left (app. K90). This was completed by 8 p.m. by the Battalion, without losses. At night the new line was reorganised and dispositions made.	" K89 " K90

Army Form C. 2118.

WAR DIARY
or
INTELLIGENCE SUMMARY.
(Erase heading not required.)

Instructions regarding War Diaries and Intelligence Summaries are contained in F.S. Regs., Part II. and the Staff Manual respectively. Title pages will be prepared in manuscript.

Place	Date	Hour	Summary of Events and Information	Remarks and references to Appendices
Near CHAMBRECY	1918 June 1		In sept. - two platoons (strength about 80) being out in the BOIS D'EGLISE (about the R. of CHAMBRECY. Batt HQ was established about 200 yards South of the E. in CHAMBRECY.	
	2		Nothing of importance happened during the day - shelling was intermittent. At dusk the re-organisation detailed to Brigade (in B.M. 1651/5 [App.K91]) was complete. This involved practically no movement of troops but details of the 8th Division and of 9th R.W.F. and 9th Welch Regts. came under command of the 9th Cheshire - the whole composite battalion being commanded by Major WILLIAMS DSO, MC, 9th R.W.F. Patrols were sent out.	App. K91
	3		Quiet day. Further re-organisations were carried out at night. A company of the 5th S.W. Borderers being sent up to relieve the details of the 8th Division was proceeded to NAPPES. The 9th Cheshire Regt. now consisted of all 9th Cheshire formed into one company of four platoons, and one attached company of 5th S.W.B. to whole under App K92 the Command of Capt. R.H. GRIFFITHS. Patrols went out and	App. K92

WAR DIARY
or
INTELLIGENCE SUMMARY.

(Erase heading not required.)

Army Form C. 2118.

Instructions regarding War Diaries and Intelligence Summaries are contained in F. S. Regs., Part II. and the Staff Manual respectively. Title pages will be prepared in manuscript.

Place	Date	Hour	Summary of Events and Information	Remarks and references to Appendices
MONTAGNE de BLIGNY	1918 June 3		finding no signs of the enemy near our own lines, outposts were established in accordance with B.M. 189/5 & B.M. 190/5 (App. Kq3) One post was however withdrawn at dawn.	(App. Kq3)
	4		Intermittent shelling during the day. The enemy guns had been showing a slight increase in activity each day (presumably as targets were discovered). A warning was received that indications pointed to an enemy attack on the morning of the 5th. Precautions were taken, protective patrols being sent out and a special stand to ordered. (App. Kq4) Similar patrols were sent out as last night (App. Kq5) and about of the enemy was located with small work due North of the MONTAGNE de BLIGNY	" Kq4 " Kq5 "
	5		Enemy artillery very active, but no concentrated shoot was carried out. At dusk the attached Company of S.W. Bdrs. was ordered to leave the Battalion and marched away about	
		10. p.m	A readjustment of the front line took place — the 9th Cheshire Regt. taking over half the left Company frontage of the 8th N. Staffs.	(App. Kq6)

M.45 Wt. W14422/M1065 35,000 12/16 D.D.&L. Forms/C/2118/14.

Army Form C. 2118.

WAR DIARY
or
INTELLIGENCE SUMMARY.
(Erase heading not required.)

Instructions regarding War Diaries and Intelligence Summaries are contained in F. S. Regs., Part II. and the Staff Manual respectively. Title pages will be prepared in manuscript.

Place	Date	Hour	Summary of Events and Information	Remarks and references to Appendices
MONTAGNE de BLIGNY	1918 JUNE 2		on our right. Patrols were sent out and the patrol detailed to investigate the suspected enemy post on the small wood (discovered last night) came into contact with about ten of the enemy here, several shots were exchanged + two Germans being killed. This was about midnight.	
		6	At 3.a.m the enemy put down a heavy barrage on the positions occupied by the Brigade on the immediate right of the Brigade front. This gradually spread to the left and by 3.30 a.m the Battalion area was being subjected to the barrage-fire. The enemy was shortly afterwards observed to be advancing to the attack in a South Westerly direction covering fire also being given to his Machine Guns from both flanks. Many casualties were inflicted on him by rifle, Lewis Gun and Machine Gun fire. He succeeded however by 7 a.m in driving the French out of the village of BLIGNY and into the BOIS de REIMS. This left the Brigade right flank completely exposed. The Bn. Staffs therefore formed a defensive	

WAR DIARY or INTELLIGENCE SUMMARY

Army Form C. 2118.

Place	Date	Hour	Summary of Events and Information	Remarks and references to Appendices
MONTAGNE de BLIGNY	1918 June 6		flank by withdrawing to the road (about the letter E of CHAMBRECY - reference map SOISSONS 1/100,000) by attacking in large numbers the enemy contrived to eject our front line troops and gain possession of their trenches. The Commanding Officer immediately issued orders for a counter-attack and Lieut's Clarke and Berry reorganised their men and assisted by the supports launched a counter-attack up the southern slopes of the MONTAGNE. This attack was held up by heavy machine gun fire before reaching the final objective and did not succeed in turning the enemy out in spite of flanking tactics that Lieut Clarke organised. The parties were compelled to withdraw and took up a defensive position on the road, immediately south of the MONTAGNE de BLIGNY. The enemy had by now (10 a.m.) strong forces in our late front line and attempts to advance all his efforts were harassed, frustrated by fire from the line on the road. About 10.30 a.m. orders were received that the hill must be Appx'or	

WAR DIARY
INTELLIGENCE SUMMARY.
(Erase heading not required.)

Army Form C. 2118.

Instructions regarding War Diaries and Intelligence Summaries are contained in F. S. Regs., Part II. and the Staff Manual respectively. Title pages will be prepared in manuscript.

Place	Date	Hour	Summary of Events and Information	Remarks and references to Appendices
MONTAGNE de BLIGNY	1918 June 6		held at all costs. The Commanding Officer commenced reorganising for further counter-attacks and at 12.30 p.m. the rescue battalion, the 1/4th K.S.L.I. arrived to assist the counter-attack, were duly launched about 1 p.m. — the details of the 8/N. Staffs were on the right - those of the 9 Cheshire in the Centre and the 1/4th K.S.L.I. on the left. Before the objective, own front line, was reached the K.S.L.I. and the N.Staffs had orders to stand fast until arrival of French troops; this they did and took up positions on the Southern and Eastern slopes of the hill. The Cheshire party pushed forward however, and on reaching the crest of the hill, where they came under heavy fire from the enemy established in our old front line, charged and recaptured our positions at the point of the bayonet. Two machine guns and 50 prisoners were taken and passed down through the K.S.L.I. This charge was led by Lieut. CLARKE — Lieut. BERRY (who was missing after the action). 2nd Lieuts. WRIGHT and LEES also took part and	

WAR DIARY
or
INTELLIGENCE SUMMARY.
(Erase heading not required.)

Army Form C. 2118.

Place	Date	Hour	Summary of Events and Information	Remarks and references to Appendices
MONTAGNE de BLIGNY	1918 June 6		amongst the men were N.C.O.s and men of other units, who had become attached to the battalion. The situation on the Batn. right was now completely restored and remained intact from this time onwards. On the left, however, the enemy still retained a hold in our trenches and attempts were made by small parties of the K.S.L.I. to get into close touch with him. The Commanding Officer took a small party up the Western slope of the hill to try and eject the enemy but hostile fire was too heavy and the party practically wiped out. He again organised two parties to attack this left flank; one was led, very gallantly, by 2nd Lieut JONES (G.H.Welsh) but was unsuccessful, the officer being wounded; the other Captain Griffiths himself led and succeeded in capturing a small portion of the trench, killing several of the enemy and wounding others - the remainder fled. The attacking party, accompanied of all units remained in occupation of this post. The	

WAR DIARY or INTELLIGENCE SUMMARY.

Army Form C. 2118.

Place	Date	Hour	Summary of Events and Information	Remarks and references to Appendices
MONTAGNE de BLIGNY	1918 June 6		enemy also held one post in the small pine wood on the left of the hill. The situation at 7.30 p.m. was as stated in the Commanding Officer's report (App K.99.) and remained unaltered.	App K 99
			About 8.0 p.m. orders were received that the Brigade would be relieved by the 150th Composite Brigade that night, the 6/7th June. The situation was now becoming quiet and by dusk all was quiet on the Brigade front. Stretcher parties were able to get to work and many wounded were brought in. Guides were despatched (as detailed in 9/44. App K100 (a).) to meet the incoming unit, the 15/H Composite Battn., and this battalion arrived in the line at 11.30 p.m. Owing to the darkness of the night the relief took some time to carry out and was not	App K100 (a) App K100 (b)
	7		completed until 2 a.m. (App K100 (c)) The Battalion moved by platoon parties to the neighbourhood of BULLIN – where the whole assembled and proceeded as a battalion to the bivouac area in the BOIS DE COUTRON. This was reached by	App K100 (c) App K100 (c)

WAR DIARY
or
INTELLIGENCE SUMMARY.
(Erase heading not required.)

Army Form C. 2118.

Place	Date 1918. June	Hour	Summary of Events and Information	Remarks and references to Appendices
Bois de COUTRON	7	4.15 a.m	(App K100 (A). Rations were awaiting the Battalion there and breakfasts were served to the men. The Brigade was now in Divisional Reserve (App K101). The day was spent in rest and cleaning up the casualties sustained by the Battn. On the 6th were found to be 2 officer, Lieut. B. BARR missing, Lieut C.H. JONES wounded, and 91 other ranks. Notification was received that the surplus personnel left behind on the 28th May was now situated in the neighbourhood of VERTUS (App K102). About 30 men who had become detached from the Battalion and done duty with other units rejoined the Battalion. T/Lieut Col. R. R. Raymer, DSO (Royal Militia of Canada) attached West Riding Regt. arrived and took over command of the Battalion.	App K100(A) App K101 App K102.
	8		A Brigade Parade was held and the Divisional Commander presented to Officers and Other Ranks the Croix de Guerres awarded by General Pelle, Commanding 5th French Army Corps, for gallantry on the MONTAGNE de BLIGNY on the 5th June. The	

Army Form C. 2118.

WAR DIARY
or
INTELLIGENCE SUMMARY.
(Erase heading not required.)

Place	Date	Hour	Summary of Events and Information	Remarks and references to Appendices
BOIS de COURTON	1918 June 8		Following were the recipients in this Battalion: With Salms Capt R.A.T. GRIFFITHS who was the first recipient. With Star - 2nd Lieut H.O. WRIGHT.	
			No. 12053 Sgt R. HAZEL, No. 25401 Sgt. J. Burley	
	9.		The Brigade was ordered to form a composite Battalion (App No 3).	App No 3
			The Battalion accordingly formed a composite company, strength 5 Officers 243. Other ranks. Officers: Capt R.H. HASLAM (Comdg Coy) Platoon Commanders: 2nd Lieut W.H. LEES, A Platoon - 2nd Lt C.R. PAINTER, B Platoon - 2nd Lieut T. WILKINSON, C Platoon - Lieut R. KERSHAW, D Platoon. Certain HQ Staff were provided as follows: Signalling Officer Lieut E. SIMCOCK, Actg Adjutant, 2nd Lt C. PLATT, M.C. 5 Signallers, 2 Runners; a watercart, cooker & 2 Lewis Gun limbers were also provided. The remainder of the battalion (i.e. 1st Q Staff) proceeded to the Transport	
FORET de REIMS			lines just North of HAUTVILLERS in the FORET de REIMS. Capt Haslam, Lieut Kershaw, 2nd Lieuts Platt and Wilkinson being with the surplus personnel near VERTUS - Lieut Black and 2nd Lieut Wright were left behind to carry on until such time as these officers rejoined the battalion to take on the duties but the Coy Cmdt	

WAR DIARY
or
INTELLIGENCE SUMMARY.
(Erase heading not required.)

Army Form C. 2118.

Place	Date	Hour	Summary of Events and Information	Remarks and references to Appendices
FORET de REIMS	June 1918 10		Transport moved south of the River MARNE to the rifle butts - 1½ miles S.E of EPERNAY. H.Q. Personnel remained with FORET de REIMS. 2nd Lieut C. Platt rejoined from Surplus Personnel and proceeded to join the Composite Batn. in the BOIS du COUTRON	
	11		All Surplus Personnel, strength 5 Officers 102 other Ranks rejoined the Battalion - being conveyed from VERTUS by motor lorry. Capt R.H.H.SLATER, Lieut R.H.STATHAM, 2nd Lieut J. WILKINSON proceeded to the BOIS du COUTRON and joined the Composite Battalion	
	12		40 Other Ranks Surplus Personnel proceeded as reinforcements to join the Composite Battalion. Remainder of Surplus Personnel formed 3 Classes :- N.C.O's Class, Lewis Gun Class, Drill Class - and carried out training in the FORET de REIMS. A Signalling Class and Scout class were also formed at the TRANSPORT LINES. The Composite Battalion relieved the 15th Composite Battn. in the front line on the night 12/13th June. Lieut. G.W.RICHARDSON (3rd R.W. Cheshire Regt. and 2nd Lieut W.DARWEN (Cheshire Regt attached) reported arrival for duty having been posted to the Battn. from J. B. D.	

WAR DIARY
or
INTELLIGENCE SUMMARY.
(Erase heading not required.)

Army Form C. 2118.

Place	Date	Hour	Summary of Events and Information	Remarks and references to Appendices
FORET de REIMS.	1918 June 14		Training classes at Battn. H.Q.	
	15		do	
	16		Church Parades at Bn. H.Q. Capt S.A. ALEXANDER and 2nd Lieuts. W.A.C. DANEY and A. THÉRIN rejoined the Battalion from C.I.B.D. on discharge from hospital.	
	17		Training classes at Battn. H.Q.	
	18		do The Composite Battn. of the 56th Brigade was relieved in the line by the Italians on the night 18/19th and in accordance with 56th Brigade Administrative Instructions No.11	App. K103.
			The Composite Company from the Battalion rejoined Battn. H.Q. and the the Surplus personnel in the FORET de REIMS, arriving about	
	19	3 a.m. A warning order was received in the store Brigade Instructions (para 3) that the Brigade would move to LE MESNIL by march route on the 20th and to the MONDEMENT area by lorry on the 21st. Billeting parties were dispatched in accordance with 26th Bde. S.C. 948/Q (App K104)	App K104.

Army Form C. 2118.

WAR DIARY
or
INTELLIGENCE SUMMARY.
(Erase heading not required)

Place	Date	Hour	Summary of Events and Information	Remarks and references to Appendices
FORET de REIMS	1918 June 20		The Battalion moved off in accordance with Brigade Order No 127 (App K.105 a) at 4.50 a.m. and marched to LE MESNIL where billets were arranged for the night. This move was completed by 11 a.m.	App K105 (a) "K105 (b)
LE MESNIL			General PELLÉE, Commanding the French 5th Corps, presented the Croix de Guerre to the 55th Infantry Brigade and is certain Officers and Other Ranks of the Division. This ceremony was carried out on the "PLACE" LE MESNIL. Copies of the "Mention" of the French Corps Orders were received (App K106)	App K105 " K106
	21		The Battalion moved by motor lorry into billets in REIMS embussing at 5.45 a.m. and reaching billets by 8.45 a.m. The Transport moved by march route starting at 9.3 a.m. and arriving about 6.30 p.m. The remainder of the day was spent in inspections and cleaning up.	" K107
REIMS	22		Training. 10 Officers and 353 Other Ranks of the 10th Cheshire (that Battalion being disbanded) joined the Battalion as reinforcements.	" K108

Officers: Major J.A. Simmons D.S.O. MC. Lieut. C. COTTERILL (7th) Lieut R.N. HALL
2nd Lieuts. G. WNUGHES (164th) E.N. WATKINS S. ADLER
J. SUGDEN (Suffolk) E. JONES (7th) F. SHARPLES (Man. Regt.)
J. SIDDONS (Ches. Regt.)

WAR DIARY
INTELLIGENCE SUMMARY.
(Erase heading not required.)

Army Form C. 2118.

Instructions regarding War Diaries and Intelligence Summaries are contained in F. S. Regs., Part II. and the Staff Manual respectively. Title pages will be prepared in manuscript.

Place	Date 1918	Hour	Summary of Events and Information	Remarks and references to Appendices
REUVES	June 23		Church Parades. Major J.A. BUSFEILD (Res. of Offs.) Cheshire Regt. reported arrival for duty from C'. I.B.D. and took over duties of Second in Command.	
	24		Training. The Battalion moved into billets in BROUSSY-LE-PETIT. Starting off at 3.30 pm and completing the billeting by 3.55 pm. Lieuts. W.F. LINDSELL (5th), A. STOCKDALE (5th) C.H.B. SEEL (5th) reported arrival for duty from C'. I.B.A.	App K 109
BROUSSY-LE-PETIT.	25		Training.	
	26		.do.	
	27		.do.	
	28		.do.	
	29		Training. The Divisional Commander (Brig. Gen. N.P. MONKHOUSE, C.M.G, M.V.O.) Divl. Artillery commanding during the absence of the 9.O.C, inspected the Transport. Two Companies of the Battalion attended a trench bullet demonstration (App K111). An advance billeting party was sent forward to BANNES.	App K110 " K111 " K112

WAR DIARY
or
INTELLIGENCE SUMMARY.
(Erase heading not required.)

Army Form C. 2118.

Place	Date	Hour	Summary of Events and Information	Remarks and references to Appendices
BROUSSY-LE-PETIT	1918 June 30		The Battalion moved by march route to billets in BANNES.	App K
BANNES			The staging area, en route, for entrainment to proceed to a new army area. The march commenced at 4.15 pm and therefore was completed by 6.30 pm.	App K113

Melhuish Baynes Lt Col.
Cmdg 9th (S) Bn CHESHIRE Regt

Army Form C. 2118.

9 Cheshire Sgt

WAR DIARY
or
INTELLIGENCE SUMMARY.
(Erase heading not required.)

WD 34

Instructions regarding War Diaries and Intelligence Summaries are contained in F. S. Regs., Part II. and the Staff Manual respectively. Title pages will be prepared in manuscript.

34 E.
13 shut

Place	Date	Hour	Summary of Events and Information	Remarks and references to Appendices
BANNES	1918 July 1		The Battalion left BANNES at 4pm and marched to FERE CHAMPENOISE where	
Rly Stop			it entrained for the North.	
CHALONS			The train which took the whole Battalion and Transport left FERE CHAMPENOISE	APP. K114
		7.33 pm	at 7.33 pm. Halts were met made at US-MARINES, and at NOYELLES.	
			The Battalion detrained at MARESCHEL (between MONTREUIL and HESDIN) at	
		5.30 pm	5.30 pm 2nd inst.	
PLANQUES	2		After detraining the Battalion marched to the staging area at PLANQUES	
Left MGR JEAN II	3		reaching billets at 3 a.m. on the 3rd inst.	
WICQUINGHEM	4		The Battalion marched to Billets at WICQUINGHEM arriving at 1.30 pm	APP. K115
Left MGR CALAIS 13	5		Training	
	6		Lieut N SCARRATT rejoined the Battalion from "C" I.B.D.	
	7		Warning Order received that the 19th Division being in G.H.Q. reserve may	APP. K116
			be required to support either the XI or XIII Corps.	
			Training 100 O.R. Reinforcements arrived from "6" I.B.D.	
	8		Training. Lieut. W.H. FINDLAY joined the Battalion from "C" I.B.D.	
	9		Training	

WAR DIARY
or
INTELLIGENCE SUMMARY.

(Erase heading not required.)

Army Form C. 2118.

Place	Date	Hour	Summary of Events and Information	Remarks and references to Appendices
WICQUINGHEM	1918 July 10		Training. 5 Other Ranks Reinforcements arrived	
	11-12		Training	
	13		The Battalion moved to AMES, marching to a point 250 yards W. of EECQUEDECQUES APP. A.117 and completing the journey by bus, arriving in billets at 3.30 p.m.	APP. A.117
AMES	14		2nd Lieut. E.C. FOX reported to Battalion from C.I.B.D. 17 O.R. Reinforcements arrived	
Regimental HAZEBROUCK 5a	15		Training. Officers and N.C.O's reconnoitred Mt. BERNENCHON area with a view to counter attack contingencies	
	16-17		Training	
	18		Training. 2nd Lieut. W. KEYINGS commenced a tour in field and posted to the Battalion. 9 O.R. Reinforcements arrived	
	19		Training. Officers and N.C.O's reconnoitred the BEUVRY area with a view to counter attack contingencies	
	20			
	21-22		Training	
	23		Training "Tracer Bullet" demonstration by one platoon of the Battalion APP. A.118	APP. A.118

Army Form C. 2118.

WAR DIARY
or
INTELLIGENCE SUMMARY.
(Erase heading not required.)

Place	Date	Hour	Summary of Events and Information	Remarks and references to Appendices
AMES	1918 July 24, 25		Training	
	26		Training. 2nd Lieut. A. SPRIGGS reported his arrival from E. I.B.D. for duty.	
	27, 28, 29		Training	
	30		The G.O.C. 19th Division inspected the Battalion on the training ground at APP. K 119	
			C.7c. (Ref. Map FRANCE Sheet 44b)	
	31		Training	

Richard Henry Field
Lt Col
Commanding 9th (S) Bn Cheshire Reg.

Army Form C. 2118.

WAR DIARY
or
INTELLIGENCE SUMMARY.
(Erase heading not required.)

Instructions regarding War Diaries and Intelligence Summaries are contained in F. S. Regs., Part II. and the Staff Manual respectively. Title pages will be prepared in manuscript.

Place	Date	Hour	Summary of Events and Information	Remarks and references to Appendices
AMES	1918 Aug. 1		Training	
	2		Training. 4 ORs reinforcements arrived	
	3		Training	
	4		Training	
	5		Training. Major J A BUSFIELD proceeded to 10th Cheshire Regt.	
LOCON Sector	6		The Brigade relieved the 8th Infantry Brigade in the front line LOCON Sector on the night 6/7th August. The Battalion moved from AMES at 3.50 p.m. and proceeded by route march to SANDPIT Camp D.2.L.C. (Sheet 44 G NE) becoming the Battalion in Brigade Reserve. This move was completed by 8.45 p.m.	APP. N° K120
	7		Training. Major R H GRIFFITHS proceeded to 4/5th Bn Stoffs + Derby Regt.	
	8		Training. Reconnoitring parties from the Battalion visited the front line. 4 OR reinforcements arrived	
Support Trenches LOCON Sector	9		Training. Lieut. G. COTTERILL proceeded to R.E. Base Depot by change	
	10		The Battalion moved into the Support trenches, relieving the 4th Shropshire L.I. The move was completed by 9 p.m. without casualties. Disposition	App K 121

WAR DIARY
or
INTELLIGENCE SUMMARY.
(Erase heading not required.)

Army Form C. 2118.

Place	Date	Hour	Summary of Events and Information	Remarks and references to Appendices
Support Line Locon Sector (Ref Map Sheet 36a SE)	1918 Aug 10.		Were as follows :- Two Companies in the ABERDEEN line from W.18.c.3.8. to x.13.d.9.9. Two Companies in the PERTH line from W.18.c.1.3. to x.19.a.6.8. Battalion HQ at W.23.c.8.8. Surplus personnel and transport remained at D.24.d.5.9.	
	11		The day passed quietly. Working parties were supplied at night.	App. K/21
	12		A quiet day. Working parties were supplied as night. Our enemy sent a few gas shells over during the early hours of the morning causing 6 O.R. casualties.	
	13		The day was quiet except for intermittent gas shelling. Working parties supplied at night. Casualties from gas shelling were :- 2nd Lieut B.L. PERRY and 13 ORs. 2nd Lieut W.R.F. THOMAS reported arrival.	
	14		Quiet day. Working parties supplied at night. Casualties 8 other ranks (gas)	
	15		The day passed quietly. The enemy artillery was more active than usual a good deal of gas shelling taking place. Casualties (gas) 2nd Lt W CARRUTHERS and 6 ORs. Capt G.C. LOWRY reported arrival.	
Front Line Locon Sector (Ref Map Sheet 36a SE)	16.		The Battalion relieved the 4th Shrops L.I. in the front line, the relief being complete without casualties about 1AM on the 17.8.18. Dispositions were as follows :- Two Companies holding main outpost line x.7.b.1.9. to x.8.d.1.1. with	

WAR DIARY
or
INTELLIGENCE SUMMARY.
(Erase heading not required.)

Army Form C. 2118.

Place	Date	Hour	Summary of Events and Information	Remarks and references to Appendices
Franklins LOCON Sector	1918. Aug. 16		advanced posts along X.1.a.3.1. to X.8.a.4.7. One Company in close support about X.8.a.0.0. and one company in reserve in EDINBURGH line X.13.a.1.8. to X.13.b.7.6.	
	17		The day passed quietly. About midnight a patrol of 1 Officer and 9 other ranks with a Lewis Gun Section went out with the object of occupying house at X.1.d.4.4 (Sheet 36ºS.E.) None of the enemy were encountered and as the house was found to be unsuitable for establishing a post the patrol returned.	
	18.		Quiet day. Patrols were again sent out at night.	
	19.		Reports were received during the day indicating the movement northwestward of the enemy whose main outpost line was now along WILLOT LANE X.1.c.7.8. to X.8.b.4.7 (Sheet 36.A. S.E.). LOCON was shelled from 5 to 6.30 pm with gas shell. A patrol sent out at dawn had reported enemy still in active occupation of their line; further patrols found no sign of retirement until at 7 P.M. the Left Company reported two of their patrols had crossed WILLOT LANE and were in lines with the enemy 200 yds north of it. 8th Gloucester Regt. (57th Infy Bde.) on left were reported to have one platoon at X.1.a.4.9, another at X.1.a.9.7 and a third moving up to positions about X.1.b.5.3 in order to join up with	App. K. 123.

WAR DIARY or INTELLIGENCE SUMMARY.

Army Form C. 2118.

(Erase heading not required.)

Place	Date	Hour	Summary of Events and Information	Remarks and references to Appendices
Frontline LOOS Sector	1918. Aug. 19		and left Company at X.1.b.8.0. left 7.50 pm patrols from left company were in touch with the enemy about X.3.c.2.8. and X.2.c.4.3.; a patrol of right Company were in touch with enemy post about X.8.a.9.8.; while a patrol moving along the canal bank was twice on from lorries at X.8.b.5.5. About 8.30 pm it was reported that right Coy had occupied enemy post at X.8.a.9.8. but further progress was hindered by Machine Gun fire from X.2.c.9.x. By 9 pm both Companies were across WILLOT LAYE. Dispositions reported at midnight showed two outpost Companies holding line X.1.b.9.1. to X.2.c.4.4. hence along road to X.8.d.5.2. with two platoons of support company moved forward to original outpost line.	
	20		Before dawn on the 20th the reserve company from EDINBURGH trench was moved forward to neighbourhood of X.8.a.0.0. who position vacated by support company, the whole of which were now occupied original outpost line (X.7.b.2.8. to X.8.a.7.3.) Battn HQ moved forward to X.8.a.3.x. About 10 am trench was re-established with	

WAR DIARY
or
INTELLIGENCE SUMMARY

Army Form C. 2118.

Place	Date	Hour	Summary of Events and Information	Remarks and references to Appendices
Trenches Locon Sector	1918 Aug. 20		8th Gloucester Regt. on the left at R.32.c.5.5. The 1/5th Sherwood Foresters (139th Brigade) on the right reported holding post about X.8.b.5.6. with enemy due in position X.9a.2.1. to X.15.d.2.5. During the day further progress was made and at 6pm a piquet line was established from X.2.c.7.8 to X.2.b.6.4.; thence to R.32.c.8.1. where touch was obtained with the Battalion on the left. The Battalion on the right established a post at X.2.a.7.7. but this post was afterwards withdrawn. During the night expeditions [patrols?] were sent out and when it was necessary to put small posts along the canal bank as far back as X.8.b.4.7. to cover the exposed flank. About 7pm the right of the piquet line was heavily shelled. Battalion HQ moved forward to X.12.9.6. Casualties during the day 110th ranks.	Appx 18, 12 &
	21.		At 5am the advance was resumed with the intention of establishing an outpost line approximately R.32.b.9.5. to X.3.a.4.4. It immediately became difficult on the right by the canal bank as the enemy put down a barrage of 5.9s and opened heavy machine gun fire from the East side of the canal. By 6.30 am the left company	

WAR DIARY or INTELLIGENCE SUMMARY

Army Form C. 2118.

Place	Date	Hour	Summary of Events and Information	Remarks and references to Appendices
Snow Hill Lecoy Sector	1918 Sept 21		L.W. moved R.32.b.75 and were held up by Machine Gun fire from both flanks, especially from about R.33.a.28. The right Company were pushing slowly forward. The machine gun fire from the East of the Canal had now ceased but the enemy artillery fire was still concentrated. At 10.20 am the position was as follows: Left Company - a Lewis Gun post at R.32.b.85, Riflepit at R.32.b.73 and Riflepit from Battalion on left immediately adjacent. The remainder of the Company holding the line with left at R.32.a.77 and right at X.3.a.39. The right Company continuing the line to X.3.a.44. During the afternoon the North S. Staffords established a post on the eastern bank of the LAWE canal at X.3.a.5.3. The above position was maintained until withdrawn when the Battalion was relieved by the 8th N Stafford Regt. and withdrew into support in the PERTH and ABERDEEN lines with Bn HQ at W.27.b.3.8. Casualties during the day were 2/Lieut W.A.C. DAVEY killed Capt R.H. HASLAM wounded and 28 other ranks killed wounded + missing. Lieut A. SCARRATT MC (attached 8th N. Staffs Regt HQ) was also wounded.	Att'k K.12.C Att'k K.12.C

Army Form C. 2118.

WAR DIARY
or
INTELLIGENCE SUMMARY.
(Erase heading not required.)

Instructions regarding War Diaries and Intelligence Summaries are contained in F. S. Regs., Part II. and the Staff Manual respectively. Title pages will be prepared in manuscript.

Place	Date	Hour	Summary of Events and Information	Remarks and references to Appendices
Support Trenches	Aug 22 to 28		Battalion occupied and took over the trenches carrying working parties in trenches and training.	
	23		The Transport and Q.M. Stores moved to ST. SAYEUR (D. S. Central Belg Map N.E.)	App K125
	24		The surplus personnel moved to BUSNETTES (N. 14 + 15 B8/a Map 36ASE)	App K126
	26		Surplus Personnel joined the Transport moves from BUSNETTES to ST. SAVEUR. 14 Other ranks reinforcements arrived.	App K127
	28		Advance parties of 8th Gloucester Regt came up and reconnoitred the Battalion dispositions.	App K128
	29		The Brigade was relieved by the 57th Infy Brigade, the 8th Gloucester Regt relieving the Battalion, this relief was complete by 7PM and the Battn marched back into billets in ALLEZIN (E 9 central Belg Map 44b) N.E.	App K130 K.130 (23+b)
	30		Rest, cleaning up, baths, inspections.	
	31		Training.	
			Total Casualties for the month :- Officers 1 killed, 2 wounded, 2 wounded (GAS). Other Ranks :- killed 5, wounded 41, wounded (GAS) 34, missing 1. Total 4 officers, 81 O.Rs.	

Graham Thurgood Lieut Col
Comdg. 9th Bn. Cheshire Regt.

WAR DIARY
INTELLIGENCE SUMMARY

9 Cheshire Regt. Vol 36

Place	Date	Hour	Summary of Events and Information	Remarks and references to Appendices
ANNEZIN	1918 Sept 1		The Army Commander (Genl Sir H.S. Birdwood) attended Brigade Church Parade at CHOCQUES and distributed medal ribbons after the Service to Officers and other ranks who had been awarded decorations. 2nd Lieuts T. GREEN and S.V. KEELING reported their arrival.	
			Other rank reinforcements 9.	
	2		Training. At 3pm verbal orders were received that the Battalion would move up by bus into reserve positions known as the Divisional Front in X.2.a and b, and R.32.c and d (Ref: Map sheet 36a S.E.) Buses were later confirmed by wire and by Brigade Order No 145, and the Battalion moved off at 9.30 pm.	K.131
LOCON	3		The Battalion arrived in position at 1.15 am. Disposition as follows. Batn. HQ at LE VERT LANNE, R.2.a.0.3 (Sheet 36a S.E.) Companies in trenches A Coy X.3.a.1.9, B Coy R.32.a.7.57.0 & still at LE VERT LANNE, R.3.c.9.x.2 ar Coy HQ — A Coy X.3.a.1.9 B Coy R.32.a.7570 C Coy X.2.4.3.4, D Coy R.32.a.2.2. At 5.30am our barrage opened and at 7am Brigade were seen coming in. The attack was reported very successful.	36 E 3 whole

WAR DIARY
or
INTELLIGENCE SUMMARY.
(Erase heading not required.)

Army Form C. 2118.

Place	Date	Hour	Summary of Events and Information	Remarks and references to Appendices
LOCON	1918 Sept 3	2.15 PM	A warning order was received from Brigade to be prepared to relieve 58th Brigade on the 4/9/18. Advance parties were sent forward to obtain billets for the night	
	4	11 AM	The orders to relieve the 58th Brigade were cancelled and information received that the Brigade would relieve the 139th Brigade.	
			2nd Lieut. J.H.B. YOUNG M.C. reported his arrival. 50th reinforcements arrived	
	5		Brigade orders No. 2/147 were received at 8 am confirming 11 store was received.	K 132
			Coy Comdrs Conference was held at 10.30 AM. The Battn moved off at 3 PM and after a halt for tea arrived at WINDY CORNER (S.9.a. 6.9. Sheet 36 Sw) at 7 PM. where guides were met. The Battn waited until 9.30 PM and then proceeded by Sections up the line to relieve the 9th Battn Notts	
RICHEBOURG	6		& Derby Regt. Relief was completed by 12.30 AM. East F.C. LOWRY (wounded) 2nd Lieut MOLYNEUX and Lieut MILBOURNE reported their arrival. There was considerable shelling during the night with a few gas shells at 4.30 AM. At 4.30 AM he was many put down a barrage in return which lasted until 5.15 AM. The NAM. Card D Coy patrols visited SALLY TRENCH	

WAR DIARY
or
INTELLIGENCE SUMMARY.
(Erase heading not required.)

Army Form C. 2118.

Place	Date	Hour	Summary of Events and Information	Remarks and references to Appendices
RICHEBOURG	1918. Sept 6.	—	SAPPER TRENCH & SALAD TRENCH reaching no opposition. Our line now runs as follows: 2 platoons of C.Coy. hold line 50yds. W. of LA BASSEE Road from SALLY to MITZI Trench thence along MITZI trench to S.11.c.2.3 (Sheet 36 SW) 2 platoons D.Coy. hold from S.11.c.2.3 along MITZI trench to approx. S.16.d.1.7 where the line was continued South by 8th Bn. N. Staffords Regt. They pushed forward a post to S.17.a.2.9. There were frequent hostile aeroplanes	
			over our lines for the day. 2 other O.R.s wounded for duty today. Day passed quietly with the exception of intermittent shelling of area	
	7		S. g. 4. from 6A.O.I. to 10.30 a.m.	
	8		Fairly quiet day with occasional gas shelling	
			At 4pm Operation Orders from Brigade were received. [...] of the operation was to advance the line to run through DE TOURETTE Fm. in front of QUINQUÉ to where it crossed the LA BASSEE Road. This to be carried out on the morning of the 9th. Casualties today 1 O.R. wounded.	K133
	9		At 7.30 am the Ghurkhas were relieved. Day passed quietly. Reconnoitred posts of the 4th R. Shrops.L.I. arrived at 11am	

WAR DIARY
or
INTELLIGENCE SUMMARY.
(Erase heading not required.)

Army Form C. 2118.

Place	Date	Hour	Summary of Events and Information	Remarks and references to Appendices
RICHEBOURG ST VAAST	1917 Sept 9		Battalion were relieved by the 4th K.S.L.I. and relief was completed by 11 P.M. The Bns. withdrew to Portuguese line of support and rear to Portuguese line at 3 A.M. Casualties for the day 1 O.R. wounded	K132
	10		Day passed quietly. Two companies bathed and working parties found supplies. Casualties for day 2 O.R.s wounded — 10 O.R. reinforcements.	
	11		Two minutes of both taken. Usual working parties and supplies. Quiet day. Reinforcements — 2 O.R.s joined.	
	12		Fairly quiet day. Enemy 5.9s fire by batt. HQ during night. Workmen parties found. Casualties for day 1 O.R. wounded.	
	13		Quiet day. Reconnoitring party proceeded to 8th N. Staffs R.s in right batn sector. The Battalion relieved the 8th N. Staffs Regt. Relief was complete by 10.55 PM. Casualties for day 2 O.R.s killed.	K134
	14		Day passed quietly. Patrols were found along Railway towards DE WITLOTTE Fm. but later driven back by M.G. fire. 1 O.R. big killed. A patrol also pushed along NORA TRENCH was shouted by the enemy. 2 officers and 1 wounded, and 1 O.R. . The two officers were 2/Lieut. E.A. PORTER and E. OLDERSHAW.	

WAR DIARY or INTELLIGENCE SUMMARY

Army Form C. 2118

Place	Date	Hour	Summary of Events and Information	Remarks and references to Appendices
RICHEBOURG	1916 Sept 15		Our Artillery carried out a short N.W. and N. of SHEPHERDS REDOUBT. A patrol of 1 NCO and 2 men proceeded to reconnoitre vicinity of SHEPHERDS REDOUBT and returned without being perceived. 3 O.R's reinforcements joined.	
	16		At 7.30 p.m. the right Coy (A Coy) under cover of artillery and M.G. barrage attacked DE TOULOTTE Fm. They encountered wire opposition and little third objective dotted casualties. The left Coy (B Coy) should have attacked knee junction at S.16.d.8.7 at the same hour but owing to our barrage dropping short they were unable to advance. Casualties for day :– Lieut (A/Capt) W.H.FINDLAY MC. wounded, 2 ORs killed, 30 OR wounded. Battalion was relieved by the 10th R. Warwick Regt. relief was complete by 10.10 p.m. On relief Bn proceeded to LA MOTTE. (F.1.b.8.4).	K135
LA MOTTE	17		The Battalion rested. Coys carried on with kit inspections etc.	
	18		Training. Battalion was allowed baths. Musical Officers inspection. 10 R's joined.	
	19		Training. Thorough practice provided under R.E. supervision.	
	20		Training. Orders received for the Brigade to relieve the 58th Brigade in the left sector on the 22nd inst. Officers reconnoitred his line of relief and left sector.	

Army Form C. 2118.

WAR DIARY
or
INTELLIGENCE SUMMARY.
(Erase heading not required.)

Instructions regarding War Diaries and Intelligence Summaries are contained in F. S. Regs., Part II. and the Staff Manual respectively. Title pages will be prepared in manuscript.

Place	Date	Hour	Summary of Events and Information	Remarks and references to Appendices
LA MOTTE	1918. Sep 21		The Battalion proceeded in buses at 8 A.M. to 1st Army Training Area, BEUVRY and carried out scheme to Frontage. 2nd Lieut J. WILKINSON proceeded to England to join R.A.F.	
	22		Church Parade 11.30 A.M. At 2 P.M. the Battalion proceeded to the trench return trip Sector to relieve the 9/K.O.Y.L.I. Machine Relief was	K 136
LA COUTURE			complete by 6.55 P.M. 2nd Lieut T. GREEN returned from XIII Corps Gas School. 5 O.R. reinforcements joined.	
	23		Working parties were formed, under R.E. supervision. Day Quiet. 2nd Lieut E.N. WATKINS returned from XIII Corps Infantry School. 2nd Lieut I. ATHERIN reported his arrival.	
	24		Lt.Col. R.R. RAYNER D.S.O. proceeded to Centre with C.R.E. Day fairly Quiet. Usual working parties found. Baths allotted to Battn at VIEILLE-CHAPPELLE.	
	25		Day Quiet. Reconnoitring parties went forward to NIEPPE Sector. Orders received to relieve 8/N. Staffords in the line. 2 O.R. reinforcements joined.	
	26		Working parties under R.E. supplied. Battalion relieved the 8/N. Stafford Regt. in the	

Army Form C. 2118.

WAR DIARY
or
INTELLIGENCE SUMMARY.
(Erase heading not required)

Instructions regarding War Diaries and Intelligence Summaries are contained in F. S. Regs., Part II. and the Staff Manual respectively. Title pages will be prepared in manuscript.

Place	Date	Hour	Summary of Events and Information	Remarks and references to Appendices
NEUVE CHAPELLE SECTOR	1916		Relief in Sub Sector left Sector. Relief was complete by 11 P.M. Fairly quiet day.	K.23
	27		Fairly quiet all day. Patrols pushed out with object of establishing post in old German front line. These were unsuccessful.	
	28		At 12 Mn One platoon of D Coy attacked the enemy Outpost line at S.5.T.5.1. Enemy machine gun fire encountered, and one prisoner captured. Casualties: 1 OR. killed, 3 ORs wounded & 2 ORs missing.	K.130 Appx 2.K.120
	29		Day fairly quiet but enemy artillery became active during evening, shelling POST KEGG heavily. Our patrols found the enemy to be alive holding his front line. Casualties: 1 OR killed, 2 OR. wounded.	
	30		Enemy activity quiet. Enemy posts were established at M.36.c 55.90 & M.36.c.75.90. Patrols found enemy line still occupied on the left. During the night an inter Coy relief was carried out. A Coy relieving D on the right and B Coy relieving C on the left. Lieut Col P.R.Rayner D.S.O. proceeded to the 51st SnK Warehouse to take command.	

C. J. Moof Lieut. Col.
Comdg. 9th Bn. Cheshire Regt.

WAR DIARY
or
INTELLIGENCE SUMMARY.
(Erase heading not required.)

Army Form C. 2118.

Place	Date	Hour	Summary of Events and Information	Remarks and references to Appendices
NEUVE CHAPPELLE	1918. 1st Oct		Artillery and M.G. average very active all day. The enemy was found to be holding SANDY TRENCH by our patrols. Reconnoitring party of 5 Officers and 17 NCOs of the 10th Bn. Kings Shropshire L.I. 2/Lieut Daniels of the 10th K.S.L.I. wounded whilst reconnoitring. Casualties for day 1 Oh wounded.	
	2nd.		At about 09.00 hrs the enemy was found to have evacuated his front system of trenches. A Coy on the left of the Battalion front and B Coy on the right pushed forward through the enemy trench systems. A Coy reaching the AUBERS Ridge by 11.00 hrs. 'B' Coy being later on account of having to clear BOIS de BIEZ. Touch was not gained with the enemy but the following positions were taken up to enable the Battalion to be relieved by the 10th KSLI. (Sheet 36 SW) N.33.b.4.0 – extremity on Battn left flank, line running along western side of Road running SW from the front through WICART Fm, LA CLIQVETERIE Fm joining trench running S.E. at T.3.a.o.o as far as L'AVENTURE which was the extremity of Bn front on the right flank. The Battalion was relieved during the night by the 10th K.S.L.I.	K 140

WAR DIARY
or
INTELLIGENCE SUMMARY.
(Erase heading not required.)

Army Form C. 2118.

Place	Date	Hour	Summary of Events and Information	Remarks and references to Appendices
NEUVE CHAPELLE	1918. 2 Oct.		at the 74th Division. Lieut.Col. C.F.KING DSO. MC. arrived and assumed command of the Battalion.	
			H. Coy. found for duty. Remainder Friday hill.	
RAIMBERT. 3rd.			Relief was complete by 01.10 and the Battalion assembled at PONT LOOP where buses were waiting, arriving at RAIMBERT at about 08.30 hours.	
			Remainder of day the Battalion rested & cleaned up.	
	4th.		Battalion received orders that the Division was to proceed to the Third Army.	K141
			The Battalion left billets in RAIMBERT at 12.45 hours and entrained at COLONNE RIQUART at 15.30 hrs. After a journey of about 5 hours the Battalion detrained at SAULTY (LENS II) and marched to billets in COUTURELLE arriving here at 21.00 hours. Batn. H.Q. was situated	
COUTURELLE	5th.		in the Chateau. The Battalion was allotted tasks in the area and was occupied away	
	6th.		the day in cleaning up. 60ths arrived reinforcements. Battalion carried out training in the vicinity of billets. Brigade order was received that the Brigade group would move on the 7th next.	

WAR DIARY
or
INTELLIGENCE SUMMARY.
(Erase heading not required.)

Army Form C. 2118.

Place	Date	Hour	Summary of Events and Information	Remarks and references to Appendices
COUTURELLE	1918 6.Oct		to the GRAINCOURT Area by bus.	
	7th		The Battalion entrained at SAULTY at about 11.00 hrs. arriving in GRAINCOURT Area at about 20.00 hours. Battalion being in bivouac in square E.24.b. (Sheet 57c)	K142
			Capt. A.J. GATELEY proceeded to report to Town Major DOULLENS for duty as a Town Major. 2nd Lieut. A. THERIN admitted to Field Ambulance.	
GRAINCOURT	8th		Remained in the Camp.	
	9th		The Battalion moved to camp vacated by 10th Bn. Royal Warwick Regt. the 57th Brigade in square E.29.a. (Sheet 57c) On moving from E.24.b to E.29.a the Battalion practised the attack in square formation with E.29.a as the objective. They closed on the camp. At 13.10 hrs message was received from Brigade that the Battalion would move at 15.00 hrs to PROVILLE. Battalion arriving in PROVILLE at 18.55 hrs. Battalion H.Q. located at A.20.b.5.2.(Sheet 57 F)	K143
PROVILLE	10th		2nd Lieuts W.R. REARDON and H. PERTIGO arrived. 10R. Reinforcement Reported.	K144
	11th		Battalion were engaged clearing up the Battlefield of bodies and wreckage.	

WAR DIARY
or
INTELLIGENCE SUMMARY.
(Erase heading not required.)

Army Form C. 2118.

Place	Date	Hour	Summary of Events and Information	Remarks and references to Appendices
PROVILLE	1918. 12 Oct		The Battalion moved at 16.00 hours to Faub^g du PARIS arriving there at about 17.30 hours. Battn HQ located at A.22.a.6.6. (sheet 57.f).	K.147.5
	13th.		2/Lieuts D.P. HUDSON and J. BOOTH arrived for duty. Battalion training. Practised taking up position of assembly for the attack outside the village.	
	14th.		Church services were held. Battalion cleaning area of Bath Houses, salvage etc.	
	15th.		Training. Battalion lectured on letter received by Battalion Pioneers. At 17.15 hrs. had a warning order was received that the Brigade would move to AVESNES on the 17th inst.	
	16th.		The Battalion carried out a tactical scheme. The 3rd Staffordshires providing one Coy. to act as Enemy. Battn returned to billets at 13.30 hrs. Lieut C.H. JONES left the Battalion to take out duty as Town Major, AWOIGNT.	K.147.6
	17th.		Battalion moved from Faub^g du PARIS to AVESNES LEZ AUBERT. The move commenced at 11.00 hrs. the Battalion as advance guard to the Brigade. The route taken was across country. Battalion halted for dinner at	K.147.7

Army Form C. 2118.

WAR DIARY
or
INTELLIGENCE SUMMARY.
(Erase heading not required.)

Instructions regarding War Diaries and Intelligence Summaries are contained in F. S. Regs., Part II. and the Staff Manual respectively. Title pages will be prepared in manuscript.

Place	Date	Hour	Summary of Events and Information	Remarks and references to Appendices
AVESNES-LEZ- AUBERT	17th	13.00 hrs	The Btn. and arrived in AVESNES LEZ AUBERT at 17.00 hrs. The following transport was with the Battalion in AVESNES and the remainder including Q.M. Store at RIEUX.	
	18th		The remainder of transport to rejoined the Battalion in AVESNES LEZ AUBERT. Battalion paraded at 11.30 hours in full Marching Order for inspection. Lieut. M.M. THORBURN arrived for duty. 2 O.R.s reinforcements reported for duty.	
	19th		Training. Battalion remained in newly arranged Billeting Area at	
		11.00 hours	Advance party went at 09.00 hours to reconnoitre area W. of HAUSSY for Bivouac camp.	
			Battalion moved at 20.25 hrs. and on arrival at position S.E. of ST. AUBERT proceeded to dig in. Two Brigades (the 59th Brigade and the 58th Brigade) were to attack the enemy positions N.E. of HAUSSY early the following morning with the 56th Brigade in reserve. The Battalion being the Reserve Battalion to the Brigade.	
ST. AUBERT	20th		At 02.00 hours our barrage opened and continued very intense for about half an hour. The enemy did not retaliate in the area	

Army Form C. 2118.

WAR DIARY
or
INTELLIGENCE SUMMARY.
(Erase heading not required.)

Instructions regarding War Diaries and Intelligence Summaries are contained in F. S. Regs., Part II. and the Staff Manual respectively. Title pages will be prepared in manuscript.

Place	Date	Hour	Summary of Events and Information	Remarks and references to Appendices
ST. AUBERT	1915 20th		occupied by the Battalion. The Battalion was at one hour's notice to move.	
			At 08.00 hrs the Battalion moved forward to position about V.8.d.1.1 (Sheet 51a) and dug in. The Battalion remained in this position until about 20.45 hrs when orders were received to	K150
			move back into billets in St AUBERT. 1 O.R. Reinforcement reported.	K151
	21st		Battalion engaged cleaning up and resting.	
			1 O.R. Reinforcement arrived.	
	22nd		Battalion training in vicinity of village. Orders were received at about 15.00 hours that the Brigade would move on the 23rd instant to CAGNONCLES.	
	23rd		Baths were allotted the Battalion at St. AUBERT.	
			The Battalion moved from St. AUBERT at 10.00 hrs and proceeded across country as advanced Guard, the 2/4th Rn N Staffs Regt acting as the	K148
CAGNONCLES			enemy in rearguard action. The Battalion arrived in CAGNONCLES at 13.00 hours.	
			Major T.P. ATKINS arrived for attachment to the Battalion. 1 O.R. Reinforcement joined.	
	24th		Training in vicinity of village. At 10.30 hrs warning order was	K149

WAR DIARY
or
INTELLIGENCE SUMMARY.
(Erase heading not required.)

Army Form C. 2118.

Place	Date	Hour	Summary of Events and Information	Remarks and references to Appendices
CAGNONCLES	1918. 24th Oct		Received that the Brigade would return to ST AUBERT. Battalion moved at 14.00 hrs and proceeded by same route as from ST AUBERT to CAGNONCLES arriving in ST AUBERT at 17.30 hours. Lieut. A. ANDERSON arrived and reported for duty as Signal Officer.	
	25th		Battalion training in vicinity of village.	
	26th		The Battalion moved back to CAGNONCLES by same cross-country route arriving here at 13.00 hours. Billets were very dirty and Battalion was engaged cleaning them up.	K152
	27th		Baths were allotted the Battalion at CAGNONCLES. Battalion Church Parade held. The troops were thoroughly inspected.	
	28th		Battalion training in area S.S.E. of CAGNONCLES. Training scheme as per programme.	
	29th		Battalion Parade at 09.15 hours for presentation of Army Rifle Association medallion won by No 1st Section in March 1918. Battalion training. Signallers carried out Sphinx scheme along with	K153

Army Form C. 2118.

WAR DIARY
or
INTELLIGENCE SUMMARY.
(Erase heading not required.)

Place	Date	Hour	Summary of Events and Information	Remarks and references to Appendices
CAGNONCLES	1918. 29th.		In billets. Batallions of the Brigade. The Battalion carried out a lecture scheme on the Training Area. Lieut W.G. GUNTER arrived and reported for duty. 10 O.Rs reinforcements reported for duty. 2nd Lieut J.E. CLARKE and 2nd Lieut S.V. KEELING admitted to Field Ambulance.	
	31st.		Battalion took part in Brigade scheme of attack and various tasks in which at about 13.20 hours.	K 154

C.J. King Lieut Col.
Commanding 9th Bn Cheshire Rgt.

9th Bn Cheshire Regiment.   4:10:18.

Operation Order No. 121.

1. The Battalion will parade at 13.10 ready to move off at 13.15 with the head of the column 150 yds South East of the Cross Roads near "B" Coy billets.
   "C" Coy will parade in the PRINCE ROAD with the head of Coy at the cross Roads.

2. The Battalion will be in the order "B" Coy., Bn H.Q., C., A., D., Coy.

3. Battalion will parade closed up, but Coys will move off at distances of 100 yards.

4. O.C.Coys will at once have the Battalion starting point reconnoitred.

5. Soft Caps will be worn. Box Respirators will be carried resting on the pack.

6. Cookers will not be available for 2 days. Camp Kettles and 1 Cook per Coy with tea and sugar rations are moving by Lorry to have tea ready on the arrival of the Battalion at the new billets.

7. All men will carry full water bottles and haversack rations for consumption on the train.

                                                2nd Lieut,
                                        Asst Adjt 9th Cheshire Regt.

SECRET.   W.D   COPY No. 1.

56th Infantry Brigade Operation Order No. 158.

Reference Maps   Dated 3/10/1918.
    HAZEBROUCK 5A.
    LENS 11.

1. 19th Division (less Artillery) will be transferred from the 5th Army to 3rd Army 17th Corps on the 4th October and will be billeted in BAVINCOURT Area on arrival.

2. 56th Brigade Group for the purpose of this move will be composed as under :-

        56th Infantry Brigade.
        82nd Field Coy. R.E.
        57th Field Ambulance.
        19th Machine Gun Battn.
        No. 2 Coy. 19th Divl. Tr.

3. Transport (less portion detailed in Administrative Order to travel by train) will march on October 4th and October 5th in accordance with Administrative Instructions.

4. Personnel and portion of transport (detailed to proceed by train in Administrative Orders) will proceed by rail in accordance with Table A attached.

5. ACKNOWLEDGE.

                                        Captain,
                                  Brigade Major,
Bde. H.Q.   56th Infantry Brigade.
   GRS.

Copies to :-

1. 9/Ches. Regt.
2. 4/Shrops. L.I.
3. 8/N.Staff. R.
4. 56th T.M.Bty.
5. 82nd Fd.Coy.R.E.
6. 57th Fd. Amb.
7. 19th M.G.Bn.
8. No.2 Coy. Divl. Tr.
9. 19th Division "G"
10. 19th Division "Q"
11. 57th Inf. Brigade.
12. 58th Inf. Brigade.
13. C.R.E. 19th Div.
14. A.D.M.S. 19th Div.
15. D.A.P.M. 19th Div.
17. 19th Div. Train.
18. G.O.C.
19. Staff Captain.
20. Bde. Signal Off.
21. Bde. Transport Off.
22. War Diary.
23. War Diary.
24. File.

SECRET.   COPY No. 1.

56th Infantry Brigade Operation Order No. 159.

DATED 6/10/1918.

1. 19th Division will move to the GRAINCOURT Area by bus to-morrow 7th inst.

2. 56th Brigade Group for the purpose of the move will be composed as follows :-

   56th Infantry Brigade.
   19th M.G.Battalion.
   82nd Field Coy. R.E.
   57th Field Ambulance.

3. Embussing will take place in accordance with the attached table.
   Troops will form up in fours on the ~~left~~ *right* of the road and will be clear of the road.
   All troops will be in position by H - 30 minutes o'clock.
   H hour will be notified later.

4. Dress - Marching Order.
   Lewis guns and 12 drums per gun will be taken on the busses.
   Machine guns will be taken on the busses.

5. Units will arrange for their men to be told off in groups of 25 in order to simplify embussing.

6. Captain L. GREVILLE 9/Ches.R. attached Bde.H.Q. will supervise embussing. Each unit will send an embussing officer with the embussing strength of unit to meet Bde. embussing officer on main road opposite SAULTY Station at H - 45 minutes o'clock.

7. ACKNOWLEDGE.

                                        Captain,
                                        Brigade Major,
                                        56th Infantry Brigade.

Bde.H.Q.
 RS.

Issued through signals at 1245.

Issued to :-

1. 9/Ches. Regt.   13. C.R.E. 19th Div.
2. 4/Shrops.L.I.   14. A.D.M.S. 19th Div.
3. 8/N.Staff.R.   15. D.A.P.M. 19th Div.
4. 56th T.M.Bty.   16. 19th Div. Train.
5. 82nd Fd.Coy.R.E.   17. A.O.C.
6. 57th Field Amb.   18. Staff Captain.
7. 19th M.G. Battn.   19. Bde. Signal Off.
8. No. 2 Coy.Div.Train.   20. Bde.Transport Off.
9. 19th Division "G".   21. War Diary.
10. 19th Division "Q".   22. War Diary.
11. 57th Inf. Brigade.   23. File.
12. 58th Inf. Brigade.

SECRET.   COPY No. 1.

56th Infantry Brigade Operation Order No. 162.

Reference Map 51.A.   Dated 22/10/18.

1. 56th Infantry Brigade will move to CAGNONCLES to-morrow 23rd instant. This move will be carried out as a Brigade tactical exercise in the manner scheduled below.

2.   TACTICAL EXERCISE.

(a) 8/N.Staff.R. will fight a rearguard action from ST AUBERT to CAGNONCLES having two companies as main guard and two companies as van guard and will represent the enemy to the 9/Ches.R. and 4/Shrops.L.I. who will fight an advance guard action from ST AUBERT to CAGNONCLES.

(b) The final objective will be the high ground running from NAVES Station T.23.c.0.5. (exclusive) to road junction B.5.d.0.2. (exclusive). Upon being driven from the final objective the 8/N.Staff.R. will withdraw to CAGNONCLES CHURCH where billeting guides will meet them.
Upon the capture of the final objective (1) 4/Shrops.L.I. will assemble in T.29.a. and will meet guides at T.29.a.0.4. (2) 9/Ches.R. will assemble in B.5.a. and will meet guides at B.5.a.0.7.

(c) Boundaries for the rearguard action and the advance guard actions will be the VILLERS-EN-CAUCHIES - NAVES - CAMBRAI Road and the AVESNES - LA BAHOTTE - CAMBRAI main road (both exclusive).

(d) The advance guard action will take place with the 4/Shrops.L.I. on the right and 9/Ches.R. on the left. Boundaries between Battalions will be a line through V.13.a.0.6. - V.22.c.0.0. - U.20.c.0.0. - U.30.a.0.0. - T.28.d.0.0.

The hour of starting.

(e) 8/N.Staff.R. will be clear of the village of ST AUBERT by 0900 hours. Scouts of 9/Ches.R. and 4/Shrops.L.I. will cross the grid line U.6.c.0.0. - U.12.c.0.0. - U.30.a.0.0. at 0930 hours.

(f) Pack animals will accompany companies.
Two sections T.M.Bty. will accompany each advance guard battalion.
Dress marching order with steel helmets (with exception of 8/N.Staff.R. who will wear caps).
All further details will be arranged by Commanding Officers.

(g) 8/N.Staff.R. will wave signal flags to represent machine guns.

3. Transport will move by road in accordance with arrangements to be notified later.

4. Administrative Instructions to accompany these orders will be issued by the Staff Captain.

5. Bde. H.Q. will move independently under orders to be notified later.

6. ACKNOWLEDGE.

Issued through Signals at 14.00

                                                   Captain,
                                                   Brigade Major,
Bde. H.Q.   56th Infantry Brigade.
  GRS.

Copies to:-

1. 9/Ches.R.
2. 4/Shrops.L.I.
3. 8/N.Staff.R.
4. 56th T.M.Bty.
5. A.O.C.
6. Bde. Major.
7. Staff Captain.
8. Bde. Signal Off.
9. Bde. T.O.
10. War Diary (2)
11. 19th Division "G"
12. A.D.M.S. 19th Div.
13. D.A.P.M. 19th Div.
14. O.C. 19th Divl. Train.
15. No. 2 Coy. Divl. Tr.
16. 57th Inf. Brigade.
17. 58th Inf. Brigade.
18. File.

Army Form C. 2118.

WAR DIARY
or
INTELLIGENCE SUMMARY.
(Erase heading not required.)

Instructions regarding War Diaries and Intelligence Summaries are contained in F. S. Regs., Part II. and the Staff Manual respectively. Title pages will be prepared in manuscript.

Place	Date 1918 Nov.	Hour	Summary of Events and Information	Remarks and references to Appendices
CAGNONCLES	1st		Battalion moved at 08.30 hrs from CAGNONCLES to HAUSSY arriving there at about 12.00 hrs. The Battalion rested and took dinner there and moved off again at 15.00 hrs to SOMMAING (VENDEGIES) arriving there at about 19.00 hrs.	K155
SOMMAING	2nd		Battalion Stores, Transport and Surplus Personnel remained at SOMMAING and the Battalion moved at 15.00 hrs to the line, the Division relieving the 24th Division. The line taken over by the Battalion ran appt. as follows: from L.20.K.9.0. to L.20.a.4.9. (SLud S1.A.NE.) 'C' and 'D' Companies held the line, 'A' Company being in support and 'B' in reserve. Battalion Headquarters was located at MARESCHES B in Neuville.	
MARESCHES	3rd to 9th		Full account of operations in Appendix No. The casualties during the battle were as follows: Wounded: 2ndLieut W.R. REARDON 3/12, 2ndLieut. D.J. HUDSON E.C. FOX, S. ADLER. Lieut. W.G. GUNTER 4/12, Lieut. B. MOLYNEUX 5/12 (At 6s. 8/12), Lieut. C.H.B. SEEL, Lieut. C.R. PAINTER 6/12, 2ndLieut. T. GREEN 8/12. Other Ranks: Killed 12. Wounded 132.	K156

WAR DIARY
or
INTELLIGENCE SUMMARY.
(Erase heading not required.)

Army Form C. 2118.

Instructions regarding War Diaries and Intelligence Summaries are contained in F. S. Regs., Part II. and the Staff Manual respectively. Title pages will be prepared in manuscript.

Place	Date	Hour	Summary of Events and Information	Remarks and references to Appendices
	1918. Nov 3 9		Prisoners and guns captured by the Battalion during these operations were as follows:-	
			273 Prisoners	
			1 Field Gun 77mm	
			15 Machine Guns	
			5 Inch Mortars.	
TAISNIERES	10th		2nd Lieut. J.L. MACKENZIE reported for duty. B Coy reinforcements arrived. Battalion moved from TAISNIERES at 09.00hrs. to B.H.Q. arriving here at about 12.30hrs. Battalion HQ located at G.0.a.2.5 (Sheet 51N/4)	
	11th		Battalion carried on with clearing the area & saving, taking up equipment &c.	
	12th		Battalion continued clearing up area & cleaning up generally	
	13th		Battalion training & completing the cleaning up of area.	
	14th		The Battalion moved from B.H.Q at 09.45hrs. by march route and proceeded to SOMPAING (VENDEGIES) arriving here at about 13.00hrs.	K157

Army Form C. 2118.

WAR DIARY
or
INTELLIGENCE SUMMARY.
(Erase heading not required.)

Instructions regarding War Diaries and Intelligence Summaries are contained in F. S. Regs., Part II. and the Staff Manual respectively. Title pages will be prepared in manuscript.

Place	Date	Hour	Summary of Events and Information	Remarks and references to Appendices
SOMMAING	1918. Nov 15th		The Battalion moved from SOMMAING at 09.10 hrs. to RIEUX. Route taken was cross-country and the Battalion arrived at RIEUX at about 14.00 hrs. Battalion H.Q. was located at U.9.a.99. (Sheet 51A)	K158
RIEUX	16th		Battalion carried out Company training. Area. Football matches played in the afternoon.	
	17th		Battalion Church Parades were held for all denominations.	
	18th		Battalion spent the day in reorganisation and cleaning up also carried out musketry drill. Lieut. C.A. Jones proceeded to U.K. to report at War Office.	
	19th		Battalion paraded at 09.30 hrs. and carried out 3 hrs. training and Specialists classes. Sports during the afternoon. Lieut (A/Capt) C.H.B. Steel returned from Hospital. 2/Lieuts. W DARWIN and C. LITT reported for duty.	
	20th		Battalion parades in Battalion Bandsmen and carried on training & specialist classes for 3 hrs. Football matches &c in the afternoon.	

(A9475) W' W2158/P1150 60,000 10/17 D. D.&L. **Sch 81a.** Forms/C2118/15

Army Form C. 2118.

WAR DIARY
or
INTELLIGENCE SUMMARY.
(Erase heading not required.)

Instructions regarding War Diaries and Intelligence Summaries are contained in F. S. Regs., Part II. and the Staff Manual respectively. Title pages will be prepared in manuscript.

Place	Date	Hour	Summary of Events and Information	Remarks and references to Appendices
RIEUX	1918 Nov 21		Battalion carried out short training and commenced Educational Scheme, classes on the following subjects being formed: Elementary Education, shoemaking, tailoring, horseshoeing.	
		10.00	Reinforcements joined.	
	22		Battalion paraded at 09.30 hrs and carried out short route march. Capt. E. Watts M.C. joined the Battalion from 25th Inf. Brigade HQ.	
	23		Battalion engaged in clearing area E and SE of RIEUX.	
			Clothy parade held during the day.	
	24		Church Parade for all denominations were held.	
			Meeting party of 1 officer and 3 NCOs was despatched to CANDAS area.	
			Lieut. A.R. Robinson reported for duty.	
		11.00	Reinforcements arrived with the Battalion.	
	25		Battalion moved from RIEUX at 09.00 hrs and proceeded by march route to FAUBERG du PARIS arriving there at about 13.00 hrs.	K159
			The Battalion transport left the Battalion and proceeded direct to TALMAS, arriving at 08.00 hrs.	

WAR DIARY
or
INTELLIGENCE SUMMARY.

Army Form C. 2118.

Place	Date	Hour	Summary of Events and Information	Remarks and references to Appendices
FAUBERG DE PARIS	1918. Nov 25		The Military Medal was awarded to the following:	
			50165 Pte WSH Pollard. 43677 Pte J.N. Pickles	
			13771 - J. Barnes. 4492 - J. Shaw.	
			55233 - A.G. Smith. 14970 Sgt C. Thornton.	
			17664 - R.B. Collin. 301504 Pte E. Forster.	
			7-163 Sgt. R. Osborne.	
	26th		Battalion training carried out also Steady Drill & Specialist classes. Sports in the afternoon.	
			Lieut. H.H SUTHERLAND rejoined the Battalion for duty.	
	27th		Battalion carried out training by Companies. Battalion parade at 11.00 a.m.	
			The Military Medal awarded to No.86. Sgt. SEVERS.	
			The following Officers joined for duty:	
			2nd Lieuts. A.G. BASS, J.N. THOMAS, A.R. GUMLEY, A.D. JEFFS.	
			S.O.R. Reinforcements joined for duty.	
	28th		Battalion entrained at 09.00 hrs at FAUBERG de PARIS and proceeded via ARRAS and DOULLENS to NAOURS in the TALMAS area	K160

WAR DIARY
or
INTELLIGENCE SUMMARY.
(Erase heading not required.)

Army Form C. 2118.

Place	Date	Hour	Summary of Events and Information	Remarks and references to Appendices
NAOURS	1918 Nov 28		arrival here at about 16.00 hrs.	
	29th		Battalion engaged cleaning up equipment and titting of clothing. Swing up of Parade and Football Grounds.	
	30th		Battalion paraded on Bn. Football Ground and carried out Route march.	

J. Adimgoa Major
Comdg 9th Bn. Cheshire Regt.

SECRET.   COPY No. 1.

56th Infantry Brigade Operation Order No.165.

Reference maps Sheets 51.A., 51 combined
map already issued.   Dated 3-11-18.

1. **OBJECTIVES & BOUNDARIES.**

   (a) <u>Objectives.</u> On the 4th November 19th Division will
        attack and capture the objectives shown on the
        attached map (already issued to Battalions).
        73rd Inf.Bde. will be attacking on the right and
        the 11th Division on the left.
        The attack on the BLUE objective will be carried
        out by the 56th Inf.Bde., that on the GREEN and RED
        objectives by the 56th Inf.Bde. on the right and the
        58th Inf.Bde. on the left.
        The attacking Battalions on the left of the Brigade
        will be the 9/Welsh R.
        For attacking Battalion on the right of Brigade
        see para. 15.

   (b) <u>Boundaries.</u> Divisional and Brigade Boundaries will be
        as shown on the map already issued.
        The Inter-Battalion Boundaries will run from
        L.20.b.6.0 to L.21.a.6.6. to L.16.c.6.3. (track and
        copse inclusive throughout from the left Battalion)
        thence L.17.c.0.8 to L.17.d.5.9. to G.13.b.6.4. to
        G.14.b.21.
        The lines depicting the objectives are purely
        diagramatic. The tactical features in their neighbour-
        hood form the real objectives.
        Similarly lines showing Divisional and Brigade and
        Battalion Boundaries are only intended as a guide to
        frontages. They may always be crossed for tactical
        purposes by arrangements with neighbouring Battalions.

   (c) <u>Jumping off lines.</u> Jumping off line will run from road
        junction L.27.a.7.8. to L.21.a.1.9. to L.14.d.9.6. and
        will be marked by tape.

2. **GENERAL PLAN OF ATTACK.**

        The attack on the BLUE objective will be delivered by
   the 56th Inf.Bde. with two Battalions, each Battalion on a two
   Company front, each Company on a two platoon front. Each
   Battalion having one Company in Support and one Company in
   Reserve.
        For the attack on the GREEN objective 58th Inf.Bde. will
   pass through the Left Coy. of the Left Battalion and 56th and
   58th Inf. Bdes. will attack side by side, the 56th Inf.Bde. being
   on a two Battalion front as before.
        The attack on the RED objective will be carried out on a
   one Battalion front, the Reserve Battalion passing through the
   leading Battalion for this purpose.

3. **ARTILLERY BARRAGE.**

   (The attack will be covered by a creeping barrage of
   Field Artillery and Machine Guns. Heavy Artillery will fire
   counter battery work from Zero to Zero plus 45 minutes. After
   Zero plus 45 minutes heavy artillery will fire on selected
   localities.

   (a)   The barrage will advance at the rate of 4 minutes per
          100 yds. up to the BLUE objective.
          A pause of 30 minutes will be made when the barrage comes
          down as protector for the BLUE objective, and it will lift
          forward again at Zero plus 120 minutes.
          During the pause on the BLUE objective 58th Inf.Bde. will
          form up and deploy for their attack on the Northern portion
          of the 56th Inf.Bde. front.

- 2 -

(c) The rate of the advance from the BLUE to the GREEN
objectives will be 5 minutes for 100 yds. On arrival
at the GREEN objective a pause of half an hour will be made
during which troops will reorganise, mop up and consolidate
as detailed in para. 4.
At the end of this period the creeping barrage will cease
and the Artillery fire will be controlled by the Brigade
Commander for the purpose of the advance to the RED objective and any further fire required.

4. METHOD OF ATTACK.

(a) For the attack on the BLUE and GREEN objectives 4/Shrops.
L.I. will be the Battalion on the right, 9/Ches.R. will be
the Battalion on the left and 8/N.Staff.R. will be the
Battalion in Reserve.
The assembly line for the attacking Battalions will be
the jumping off line as detailed in para. 1.(c). The
Reserve Battalion will be concentrated about L.25.a.

(b) The attack on the BLUE objective will be carried out by
Battalions on a two company front. The Support and
Reserve Coys. will leap-frog on the BLUE objective and
proceed to the GREEN objective. 58th Inf.Bde. will pass
through the left Coy. Left Battalion on the BLUE objective
and this Coy. will then become a Reserve Company. The
mopping up of the village of JENLAIN will be carried out
by the new Support and Reserve Coys. (i.e. the original
attacking Coys.)

mopping up The Reserve Coys. after mopping up the village will
on line of 1st objective consolidate West of the River in G.13.b. and will temporarily Brigade Reserve.
Support Coys. will follow up the leading Coys. to the
GREEN objective.
Upon capture of the GREEN objective the Left Battalion
will arrange to mop up the portion of the village of
WARGNIES-le-GRAND from the North (this mopping up will
commence during the protector barrage as far as that
barrage will permit).
The Reserve Battalion 8/N.Staff.R. will pass through the
left battalion on the GREEN line North of the village and
will make good the RED objective as soon as the protector
lifts.
There will be no barrage in this attack unless desired
by Battalion Commanders or unless the troops are held up.
Heavy Machine Gun fire is being directed on to the RED
objective during the protector for the GREEN objective and
close support artillery will be ready to cover the advance
if required.

5. REORGANISATION.

Upon capture of the RED objective the Brigade will be
reorganised as follows :-
8/N.Staff.R. will be the leading Battalion and will be
distributed in depth on the RED objective and on the
Northern portion of the GREEN objective.
in depth and to 4/Shrops.L.I. will reorganise on the Southern portion
prepared to deal of the GREEN objective and will become Support Battalion.
with any counter- 9/Ches.R. will reorganise West of the road in G.14.a.
attack from S.E. and will become Reserve Battalion to the Brigade.

6. FURTHER ADVANCE.

8/N.Staff.R. will be prepared to push forward beyond the
RED objective if the enemy is found to have retired and will be
prepared to conform with either or both flanks in the event of
either of these flanks moving forward.

- 3 -

7. MAINTENANCE OF DIRECTION.

The advance to the BLUE objective will be on a True Bearing of 68°.

The advance forward of the BLUE objective will be due East.

Battalions will detail a responsible officer to be responsible for the maintenance of direction.

In order to assist in the maintenance of direction a round Thermite shell will be fired at each alternative lift of the barrage (and 200 yds. behind the latter) along the boundary to each attacking battalion up to the BLUE objective.

From the BLUE to the GREEN objective smoke shell will be substituted for Thermite.

As the barrage comes down as protector to each objective a few rounds of Thermite will be fired along the whole Divisional front.

8. MOPPING UP.

Great care is to be taken that mopping up is carefully organised before hand, definite parties will be detailed for the mopping up of definite areas, all the units including Company and Battalion H.Q. must mop up the area in which they are situated.

9. ACTION OF ARTILLERY.

Artillery barrage will be as stated in para. 3. Arrangements have been made for artillery Brigades to leap-frog forward and there will always be a large number of guns ready to cover the leading troops at any time during the advance.

Special sections R.F.A. are being detailed to move forward close behind the leading Infantry to deal with any enemy Tanks (No tanks are being used by our troops, no tanks seen or manned by the enemy).

Artillery liaison officers will be present with each Battalion H.Q. and Artillery reconnaissance parties will move forward with the leading Infantry. Details of these will be notified later.

10. ACTION OF MACHINE GUNS.

One Section of Machine Guns (C. Coy.) will move forward with each attacking Battalion to act as forward guns. The Section Commander of these guns will keep in close touch with Battalion Commanders concerned. These guns are for the purpose of assisting the leading waves by direct fire.

Two Sections Machine Guns (C. Coy.) (on limbers) will move forward under O.C. C. Coy. at Zero behind the right attacking Battalion to the high ground about point 108·2 in L.23.a. with the object of keeping the slopes on the West bank of the PETIT ANELLE under fire and also with a view to supporting a further advance on to the GREEN line.

The bridge at approximately G.7.d.4.0. will be specially engaged to prevent the passage of enemy over the River.

On the capture of the GREEN line these guns will move forward to the high ground about L.18.a.5.2. in order to engage any possible counter attack debauching from WASNIES-le-GRAND up/down the valley of PETIT ANELLE.

A and D Coys. will be dug in by Zero minus 3 hours in batches of 4 guns in a position as close as possible to the jumping off line for the purpose of cooperating in the creeping barrage.

On completion of the barrage these guns will be packed on limbers and will be held in readiness to move forward on receipt of orders.

- 4 -

After the capture of the RED line O.C. C.Coy. will coordinate the consolidation in depth of all 16 guns for the protection of the RED line.

O.C. C.Coy. will then establish his H.Q. with Battalion H.Q.

11. ACTION OF TRENCH MORTARS.

One Section Light Trench Mortars on pack animals will be attached to each attacking Battalion.

8/N.Staff.R. when leap-frogging through 9/Ches.R. will take over the 9/Ches.R. Trench Mortars.

Two Sections Light Trench Mortars on limbers will move with Brigade H.Q.

12. ACTION OF ROYAL ENGINEERS.

One Section Royal Engineers will be attached to Bde.H.Q. for the construction of Adv.Bde.H.Q. during the advance, and for any other urgent R.E. work which may crop up.

13. FLARES & LIGHT SIGNALS.

(a) Light Signals. Rifle Grenade Signals showing three REDS will be fired by the troops on reaching the BLUE objective. Rifle Grenades showing 3 Greens on reaching the GREEN objective.

The following Light Signals are being used by the Brigade on our left.

(i) White Very Lights will be fired vertically by leading Infantry to signal their arrival on any marked natural positions such as a ridge, road etc.

(ii) Red Very Lights will be fired towards any point from which the enemy is holding up the advance.

Troops are to be notified of ~~these~~ this as it may otherwise lead to confusion.

(b) Flares. A contact plane will call for flares at
Zero plus 2 hours.
Zero plus 3 hours.
Zero plus 4 hours.

The advanced troops will light flares, wave white flappers, helmets etc.

14. LIAISON.

Liaison posts on the flanks will be established at the points shown on attached map (already issued).

Each Battalion will detail mounted liaison officer and groom to report to Bde. H.Q. at ~~K.29.c.0.0.~~ by 0500 hours, 4th November.

15. ACTION OF BRIGADE ON THE RIGHT FLANK.

(a) The attack of the Brigade on the right (73rd Inf.Bde.) on the BLUE objective will be carried out by the 13th Battalion Middlesex Regt. The attack on the GREEN line will be carried out by the 7th Bn. Northamptonshire Regt. on the left. The attack on the RED objective will be carried out by the 17th Inf.Bde.

(b) 73rd Inf.Bde. have arranged to concentrate their strength on their left flank after the capture of VILLERS POL for the purpose of assisting our right flank. If trouble is experienced by us in JENLAIN or if the enemy counter attacks in or through JENLAIN 73rd Inf.Bde. have arranged to send a Battalion down the spur L.23.b. to assist us. Machine Gun assistance will also be given if required.

16. **POSSIBLE ENEMY COUNTER ATTACK.**

    (a)   It is possible that the enemy may counter attack with Tanks in which case the attack might be expected along the high ground L.5.b. and d. or from a Southerly direction through L.29.b. and L.23.d. Troops will be instructed that in case of a tank attack they are to allow the Tanks to pass through if necessary and are to fire at Infantry accompanying the tanks. The Tanks will be engaged by direct fire from close support artillery specially detailed for that purpose and by certain Machine Guns.

    (b)   Counter attacks may also develop from the villages, from sunken roads or from along the valleys. These eventualities will be dealt with by careful mopping up and by Machine Guns sited for enfilade.

    (c)   A Counter attack aeroplane will be up throughout the day.

17. **COMMUNICATIONS.**

    Visual, Runner and Pigeon communications will be maintained throughout. A Field Wireless Set will be established at the joint H.Q. of the attacking Battalions.
    It is absolutely essential that Battalions keep in touch with Brigade Report Centre.

18. **SUPPLY OF AMMUNITION.**

    Bde. S.A.A. Park and A Echelon Transport will move forward by bounds and will be located close to Adv. Bde.H.Q.

19. **S.O.S.**

    Present S.O.S. Signal is a Rifle grenade rocket Red over Green over Red.

20. **LOCATION OF H.Qs. & BRIGADE REPORT CENTRE.**

    Adv. Bde. H.Q. will be established at K.29.c.0.0. and will move forward after the capture of the BLUE objective to SAINT HUBERT L.20.central [about L.21.a] and will move forward upon the capture of the GREEN objective to the neighbourhood of L.16.central.
    Brigade Report Centre will be established before Zero at SAINT HUBERT L.20.central and will move forward upon the capture of the BLUE objective to L.16.central and will move forward on the capture of the GREEN objective to L.17.c.6.9. Both Adv. Bde. H.Q. and Brigade Report Centre will be marked by a Red flag by day and a Red Lamp by night.
    Headquarters for attacking Battalions will move forward by bounds along the inter-battalion boundary. Battalions will notify this office as early as possible the positions selected for each bound.
    O.C. Reserve Battalion will be with Adv.Bde. H.Q. until the capture of the BLUE objective, and until such time as the Reserve Battalion commences to move through the leading battalion.
    Battalion H.Q. are to be clearly marked by day and night throughout the operations.

21. **REPORTS.**

    Constant reports on the situation including even negative information are absolutely essential in order that a suitable artillery and Machine Gun protection may be given to the Infantry and in order that enemy counter attacks or concentrations for counter attacks may be dealt with.

22. STRAGGLERS POSTS & PRISONERS CAGES.

Stragglers Posts and Prisoners Cage is established at VENDEGIES. Civilians will be sent back to VENDEGIES. Forward prisoners cages and Stragglers posts will be established and their positions notified later.

23. ADMINISTRATIVE INSTRUCTIONS.

Administrative Instructions to accompany this order will be issued by the Staff Captain.

24. ZERO.

Zero hour will be 0530 hours 4th November.

25. SYNCHRONISATION OF WATCHES.

Brigade Signal Officer will arrange the synchronisation of watches at 1700 hours and 2300 hours 3rd November.

26. ACKNOWLEDGE.

Issued through Signals at

Captain,
Brigade Major,
56th Infantry Brigade.

Bde. H.Q.
3-11-1918.
GRS.

Copies to:-

1. 9/Ches.R.
2. 4/Shrops.L.I.
3. 8/N.Staff.R.
4. 56th T.M.Bty.
5. "C" Coy. 19th M.G.Bn.
6. O.C. 19th M.G.Bn.
7. 81st Fd.Coy.R.E.
8. Rt.Group R.A.(3)
9. 19th Division "G".
10. 19th Division "Q".
11. 57th Inf.Brigade.
12. 58th Inf.Brigade.
13. 73rd Inf.Brigade.
14. 32nd Inf.Brigade.
15. 57th Fd. Amb.
16. C.R.A. 19th Div.
17. C.R.E. 19th Div.
18. D.A.P.M. 19th Div.
19. A.D.M.S. 19th Div.
20. H.Q. 19th Divl. Train.
21. No. 2 Coy. Divl. Train.
22. O.O.C.
23. Bde.Major.
24. Staff Captain.
25. Bde.Signal Off.
26. Bde. T.O.
27. Lt.A.H. CARTER.
28. Bde. Intell: Off.
29. War Diary (2)
30. File.
31. O.C. Details.
32. Spare.

SECRET.

56th Infantry Brigade Administrative Instructions No.36.
Issued as an appendix to O.O. 165.
----

1. **TRANSPORT.**

    "B" Echelons of 1st line transport as laid down in this office No. S.C. 1830/Q dated 20/10/18 will be moved under Divl. arrangements until further orders.

    "A" Echelon consisting at present of 2 L.G. Limbers, 3 S.A.A. and Bomb Limbers and 1 Tool limber per Battalion is in the Railway Cutting K.34.central under Lieut. A.H. CARTER whose H.Q. are at Bde. H.Q.

    "A" Echelon will be moved forward with Bde. H.Q. as the situation permits.

2. **BURIALS.**

    All Burials will be carried out as expeditiously as possible under Battalion arrangements.

3. **AMMUNITION & FIREWORK SUPPLY.**

    Units requiring ammunition will notify this office of their requirements stating the location to which they wish it delivered and some definite landmark which can be reached by wheeled transport where guides will await it.

4. **RETURNS.**

    It is essential that returns reach Bde. H.Q. at the following hours daily -

CASUALTY RETURN	-	1600 hours.
STAND TO STRENGTH RETURN.	-	0600 hours.

5. **CLOTHING.**

    Q.M's. of Units can draw clean socks daily from the Divisional Clothing Store in HINDENBURG STRASSE,VENDEGIES.Q.8.d.4.3. provided they return an equal number of dirty socks.

6. **MEDICAL.**

    57th Field Ambulance is in charge of the evacuation of casualties from the Divisional front.
    A.D.S. is at the Chateau K.29.c.0.0.

7. **PRISONERS OF WAR & STRAGGLERS.**

    Divisional Post for Stragglers and Prisoners of War Cage is established at VENDEGIES.

    Units will send all prisoners of war to Bde. H.Q. where the Brigade H.Q. Guard will take charge of them.

    A Brigad Stragglers post will be established at the Cemetery L.25.b.6.8. tonight.

    Units will detail personnel as follows to report to the Staff Captain at Bde. H.Q. at 1800 hours today for duty at Stragglers Post and Prisoners of War Cage.

9/Ches. R.		2 men.
4/Shrops.L.I.	1 CPL.	2 men.
8/N.Staff.R.	1 Sgt.	2 men.

    They will be rationed by Brigade H.Q.

Bde. H.Q.
3-11-1918.
GRS.

Captain,
A/Staff Captain,
56th Infantry Brigade.

Copies to:-

1. 9/Ches. R.
2. 4/Shrops.L.I.
3. 8/N.Staff.R.
4. 56th T.M.Bty.
5. Bde. T.O.
6. 19th Division "Q".
7. File.
8. Staff Captain.
9. T.O. 9/Ches. R.
10. Q.M. 4/Shrops.L.I.

SECRET.   Copy No......

56th Infantry Brigade Operation Order No. 167.

Dated 9-11-1918.

Reference Map sheet 51.

1. 56th Infantry Brigade will move to BRY Area tomorrow 10th instant.

2. Route for Transport and personnel will be TAISNIERES - I.4.c. - I.19.b. - I.13.c - RUESNE - BETTRECHIES - LAPERCHE ROMPUE - BRY.

3. Units will pass Bridge at I.Y.R.1.1. at the following times:-
   "A" Echelon   0900 hours.
   9/Ches. Regt.   0915 hours.
   4/Shrops. L.I.   0930 hours.
   8/N.Staff Regt.   0945 hours.
   56th T.M.Bty.   0ff hour.
   "B" Echelon and 57th Field Ambulance will leave HOUDAIN at
   Battalions   0915 hours.

4. Infantry may move across country if they desire but must not block other units. Whilst in the road the following intervals will be maintained, between Battalions 500 yards, between companies 100 yards, between transport of units 200 yards, between every 6 vehicles 25 yards.

5. Arrangements will be made for packs from present dumps to be moved by G.S. Wagons.

6. 57th Field Ambulance will be billetted in WARGNIES LE GRAND.

7. Administrative Instructions to accompany these orders will be issued by Staff Captain.

8. Arrival in billets will be reported to Bde. H.Q. which will be located in BRY.

9. ACKNOWLEDGE.

                                                    Captain,
                                                    Brigade Major,
Bde. H.Q.   56th Infantry Brigade.
CRG.

Copies to:-
No. 1. 9/Ches. Regt.	No. 15. H.Q. 19th Div.Train.
2. 4/Shrops. L.I.	16. No. 2 Coy.Train.
3. 8/N.Staff Regt.	17. A.O.C.
4. R.M. 9/Ches.R.	18. B.M.
5. Q.M. 4/Shrops.L.I.	19. Staff Captain.
6. Q.M. 8/N.Staff R.	20. Brigade T.O.
7. 56th T.M.Bty.	21. Bde. S.O.
8. 18th Div. "G".	22. Bde. Q.M.S.
9. 19th Div. "Q".	23. War Diary.
10. 57th Inf. Bde.	24. File.
11. 58th Inf. Bde.	25. 57th Field Amb.
12. C.R.E. 19th Div.	26. 81st Field Co.R.E.
13. A.D.M.S. 19th Div.	27. Lt. CARTER
14. D.A.P.M. 19th Div.	

SECRET.   Copy No. 1.

56th Infantry Brigade Operation Order No. 168.

Reference Sheet 51 A.   Date: 13-11-1915.

1.   56th Infantry Brigade Group will move to WINNEZEELE - STEENVOORDE Area tomorrow 14th instant in accordance with Table "A" attached.

2.   Brigade Group for the purpose of the move will be comprised as under:-
            56th Infantry Brigade.
            57th Field Ambulance.
            No. 2 Coy. Div. Train.
            31st Mobile Vet. Section.

3.   Dress - Marching Order.   Transport will accompany units.

4.   Administrative Instructions to accompany these orders will be issued by the Staff Captain.

5.   ACKNOWLEDGE.

                                                    Captain,
Bde. H.Q.   Brigade Major,
GRO.   56th Infantry Brigade.

        Issued to:-
                No. 1. 9/Chesh. Regt.
                    2. 4/Shrops. L.I.
                    3. 8/N.Staff. Regt.
                    4. 56th T.M.Bty.
                    5. 57th Field Ambulance.
                    6. 31st Mobile Vet. Section.
                    7. No. 2 Coy. Div. Train.
                    8. 19th Division "Q".
                    9. 19th Division "A".
                   10. A.D.M.S., 19th Divn.
                   11. O.C. 19th Div. Train.
                   12. D.A.P.M., 19th Division.
                   13. 57th Infantry Brigade.
                   14. 58th Infantry Brigade.
                   15. S. O. S.
                   16. B. M.
                   17. Staff Captain.
                   18. Brigade Signal Officer.
                   19. War Diary.
                   20. War Diary.
                   21. File.
                   22. Bde. T.O.

SECRET.   Copy No. 1

56th Infantry Brigade Operation Order No. 169.

Reference Map 51 A.   Dated 14-11-1918.

1.   56th Infantry Brigade Group will move to RIEUX tomorrow 15th instant in accordance with Tables 'A' and 'B' attached.

2.   56th Brigade Group for the purpose of the move will be composed as under:-

         56th Infantry Brigade.
         57th Field Ambulance.
         No. 2 Coy. Train.
         61st Mobile Vet. Section.

3.   Dismounted Troops will move CLEAR OF THE ROADS.

4.   Administrative Instructions to accompany these orders will be issued by the Staff Captain.

5.   ACKNOWLEDGE.

                                                       Captain,
Bde. H.Q.   Brigade Major,
GRG.   56th Infantry Brigade.

        Copies to:-
                No. 1. 9/Ches. Regt.
                    2. 4/Shrops. L.I.
                    3. 8/N.Staff.Regt.
                    4. 56th T.M.Bty.
                    5. 57th Field Ambulance.
                    6. 61st Mobile Vet. Section.
                    7. No. 2 Coy. Div. Train.
                    8. 19th Division "G".
                    9. 19th Division "Q".
                   10. A.D.M.S., 19th Div.
                   11. 19th Divisional Train.
                   12. D.A.P.M., 19th Div.
                   13. 57th Inf. Bde.
                   14. 58th Inf. Bde.
                   15. Bde. Transport Officer.
                   16. G.O.C.
                   17. B.M.
                   18. Staff Captain.
                   19. Bde. Signal Officer.
                   20. War Diary.
                   21. War Diary.
                   22. File.

No. Z. 546

Headquarters,
56th Infantry Brigade.

Reference B.M.3878.

On the night 2nd/3rd November, the 9th Cheshire
2-11-18 Regiment took over the line. The Battalion was on the
front L.20.b.7.0. to L.20.a.4.9., two companies being
in the line, one in support and one in reserve.
During the night an officer's patrol
ascertained that the enemy was holding LA PATTE D'OIE
in L.15.b., in some strength.

08.00 hours
On the morning of the 3rd it was found
that the enemy had withdrawn and the patrols of the
Division on the left were observed to enter the FORT DE
11.00 hours CURGIES in L.9.d.
The two front companies immediately
pushed forward to regain touch. Advancing troops came
under fire from about 8 Machine Guns located on the West
edge of JENLAIN and in CHATEAU D'EN HAUT FERME as they
passed over the ridge in L.22.a. and L.15.d. This ridge
was consolidated in accordance with verbal orders
received from the G.O.C., Brigade, while strong patrols
11.15 hours pushed forward and reached the high ground in L.17.c.,
L.17.a. and L.10.d., getting into close touch with the
enemy

In the meantime the support and reserve
companies and Battn. Hd.Qrs. were moving up. On
arrival the reserve company and Bn.H.Q. were located in
the sunken roads in L.20.a. and the support company took
over the ridge in L.22.a. and L.15.d. from the two front
13.00 hours companies who then moved forward in support of their
patrols.

There was by this time a very severe
bombardment by guns of all calibres of the whole area
from Bn. H.Q. to the line established by the patrols.
The Trench Mortar Section was sent forward to support
the front companies but did not come into action.
The troops of the Division on the left
had still not advanced beyond FORT DE CURGIES and the
position of the right Battalion was obscure and
remained so throughout the day.
There was a sharp fire fight between the
front companies and enemy Machine Guns, under cover
of which one platoon of the left company pushed through
the orchards running North of the road running East
and West through L.17.a., and got into the Northern
outskirts of the village, capturing a few prisoners.
This caused the enemy on the Battalion front to withdraw and the left company advanced through the North
edge of the village and established itself on the
sunken road in L.11.d., a,d b. Touch was now
16.00 hours established by this company with the W.Yorks. of the
11th Division who had advanced to the JENLAIN - CURGIES
Road.

Meanwhile the right front company pushed
on through the village and made good the line of the
Railway - one platoon being posted at L.18.c.7.7. - a
few prisoners were taken. As there was no touch with
the right battalion, the support company simultaneously
16.00 hours moved up on the right of the right company. The enemy
was engaged in L.17.d. and L.24.a. and driven out, a
few prisoners being captured. The company then
established itself about L.24.a.3.5. with one platoon
in the sunken road at L.23.a.8.2. Nothing was known
17.00 hours of the position of the right Battalion. Bn. H.Q.

and the reserve company were now established about LA PATTE D'OIE, L.15.b.

All the above movements were carried out under very heavy shell fire from the enemy and an irritating fire from our own field guns.

4-11-18   Orders having been received for the Battalion to assemble on the JENLAIN - CURGIES Road ready to
06.00 hours   continue the advance under a barrage at 06.00 hours in accordance with Operation Order No. 165 and the Welsh Regt. having moved up, all companies were now withdrawn to the new assembly position. All men received a meal from the field kitchens.

06.00 hours   At 06.00 hours the attack was resumed with two companies in the front line, one in support, the reserve company coming under orders of Brigade. Companies kept well up to the barrage which was satisfactory. Considerable opposition was met with from the river Eastwards. Many prisoners and Machine Guns and some Trench Mortars were captured and a number of the enemy killed.

07.30 hours   On the capture of the Green Line considerable trouble was caused by our barrage falling very short. Some casualties occurred and the left company withdrew for a short time. Directly our barrage ceased this company moved forward again over it's objective and swung South down the road in L.15.a. Prisoners and Machine Guns were captured during the movement. The company came under sharp fire from L.15.a. and d. but kept this under by it's own covering rifle fire whilst it moved forward.

08.15 hours   The village was entered and mopped up. Many prisoners were taken. The whole village was cleared by
10.00 hours   10.00 hours. The company was reorganised and platoon posts established at G.15.d.75.25. and G.15.d.05.50. The company kept touch with the N.Staffords but none could be
14.00 hours   made with the 24th Division until about 14.00 hours, when information was received that they were going to attack the Red Line about 15.30 hours.

The Battalion now came into reserve with Bn. H.Q. at G.7.d.35.15. The reserve company rejoined during the evening.

5-11-18   On the 5th the Battalion moved forward to G.16.a. and c.

6-11-18   On the early morning of the 6th the Battalion again moved forward and dug-in in G.18.a. and b. with Bn.H.Q. at H.13.a.3.7.

On the night of the 6th the Battalion was lent to the 57th Brigade to assist in an attack across the river HOGNEAU. The Battalion was to attack behind the Royal Warwickshire Regt., swing North and capture and consolidate the ridge in H.11.a. and H.5.c., while one company moved North immediately after crossing the river and mopped up the railway and wood as far North as B.28.c. and d.

7-11-18   The Battalion was assembled by Zero hour
06.00 hours   (06.00 hours) in H.9.c. and H.15.a. The barrage was the worst the Battalion has ever experienced. Very thin, very short, no line, no regard to the programme of turning. Most of the howitzer shells fell behind the 18 pounder bursts.

All objectives were gained, one or two of the enemy killed and four prisoners taken. No opposition was encountered. The village of BELLIGNIES was entered and made good. Our own artillery made it a very difficult and dangerous proceeding.

The 58th and 57th Brigades now squeezed out the Battalion which returned to billets in LA FLEMENGRIE.

On the 8th the Battalion moved to I.10.a. From I.13.c. onwards it formed the left flank guard to the Brigade. Touch was established with troops of the 11th Division who were on the line of the road I.4.c. - GREUSON PIERRE FARM - C.29.a. thence Westwards. One company was put on outpost in I.5.c. and d. The remainder of the Battalion was in I.4.c. and b.

At dawn on the 9th the 11th Division advanced and the Battalion was squeezed out.

On the 10th the Battalion marched back to BRY.

I consider the chief lessons learnt or emphasized were as follows:-

1. Importance of good and quick communications.

2. Importance of the R.A.M.C. keeping close touch with the situation.
On the 3rd November a large number of casualties were stretcher cases. These had to be carried back from JENLAIN to MARECHES a distance of 6000 yards. The supply of stretcher bearers and stretchers quickly became exhausted. When the Battalion attacked on the morning of the 4th it went forward without the Medical Officer and R.A.M.C. bearers who were still trying to evacuate about 40 cases from LA PATTE D'OIE, and many severely wounded were still lying East of JENLAIN, there being no stretchers to get them away with. Valuable lives were unnecessarily lost.

3. The importance of artillery keeping in touch with progress of Battalions. Throughout operations the Battalion was hampered and casualties caused by our own artillery.

4. If the artillery have not time to ensure a reasonable degree of accuracy they had better not fire at all.

5. Against a retreating enemy, artillery prevents the attack moving fast enough to get well into the enemy and prevents exploitation of success. Also it keeps the attack in the zone shelled by the enemy.

6. The Battalion profited greatly by recent training. All Infantry and Machine Gun opposition was quickly dealt with by supporting sections pushing round enemy's flank, whilst the sections held up gave covering fire. These tactics were invariably successful.

7. The importance of keeping sections in "snakes" under the hand of the Section Commander whether opposition was encountered or not.
Section commanders could always find a covered route round the enemy's flank if they wished to advance and could get their men into fire positions if they wished to fire.

8 Importance of men using their rifles. Enemy Machine Gun and rifle fire was silenced by our rifle fire.

9. Rifle bombs were carried and all men were practised in their use, but they were not fired. I think they might have been used with advantage on several occasions. Smoke bombs were not carried, although they might have been used with advantage on several occasions.

10; Visual (lamp and flag) was used largely on the 3rd and to less extent later on when the country became more close. Shutters were used by platoons on

---4---

one or two occasions, but most of them were lost by the end of the operations.

11. In bad weather Lewis Guns should be carried in canvas bags when not firing.
Clean L.G.Ammunition should be issued in exchange for the old whenever possible.

12. Cookers should be in close touch with the Battalion ready to provide hot food wherever possible. A reserve of food with the cookers is very desirable as it is necessary to issue rations to men and these cannot be called in again and cooked.

13. A good supply of rum is essential.

Lieut.-Colonel,
Commanding 9th Bn. Cheshire Regiment.

17th November 1918.

WAR DIARY
INTELLIGENCE SUMMARY

9th Yorks Regt.

VII 39

Place	Date	Hour	Summary of Events and Information	Remarks and references to Appendices
NAOURS	1915 Dec 1-10		Billetting in NAOURS. Training, Education & Recreation.	
	11		The battalion moved into the hutment camp at VILLERS L'HOPITAL by route march, starting at 10.00 hours & arriving at 19.00 hours.	
VILLERS L'HOPITAL	12-31		Training, Education & Recreation.	

A King
Lt Col
Commanding 9th Yorks Regt

Army Form C. 2118.

F17
9 Cheshire 98 40

WAR DIARY
or
INTELLIGENCE SUMMARY.
(Erase heading not required.)

Place	Date	Hour	Summary of Events and Information	Remarks and references to Appendices
VILLERS L'HOPITAL	1 to 31 Jan.		Battalion in Camp in VILLERS L'HOPITAL.	
			Lieut. Col. KING D.S.O. M.C., Capt. E. WATTS M.C., Capt. J. H. B. YOUNG D.S.O. M.C. proceeded to England for demobilisation 4th Jan/19.	
			Major T. P. ATKINS proceeded to England for demobilisation 26th Jan/19.	
			Lieut. R. M. Hart to England sick 24.1.19.	
			62 O.Rs. Reinforcements were received during the month.	
			164 O.Rs. proceeded to England for demobilisation during month.	
			Strength of the Battalion 31.1.19. was 28 Officers 471 O.Rs.	

D Neville Capt & Major Rgt.
Comdg. 9th Cheshire Regt.

WAR DIARY
INTELLIGENCE SUMMARY

9/Cheshire Regt.

Vol 41

Place	Date	Hour	Summary of Events and Information	Remarks
Villers L'Hopital	1919 Feb 1/26th	10h.	Stationed in camp in Villers L'Hopital. H.R.H. Prince of Wales presented colours to the Battalion on a Brigade Parade. Draft consisting of the following Officers and 179 Other Ranks proceeded on the 6th inst. to join the 1/6th Bn. Cheshire Regt. for the Army of Occupation. Capt. C.J.H. Sell. Lieut. G.W. Hughes M.C. Lieut. A. Thérin M.M. Lieut. H.B. Johns Lieut. W. Darwin M.M. Lieut. J.C. Mackenzie. Lieut. H.B. Wright M.C. Lieut. J.S. Notley Lieut. A.R. Robinson. Lieut. A.R. Burnley 156 O.R's. were demobilized from the 1st to the 26th inst, 16 O.R's were demobilized whilst on leave to U.K. On the 26th. the Battalion Transport moved under orders received to CANDAS en route for transfer to the Second Army in the Army of Occupation. The available personnel of	

Place	Date	Hour	Summary of Events and Information	Remarks and references to Appendices
VILLERS FAUC L'HOPITAL	26th		14 Officers and 46 o.r.s under orders to move to the Second Army on the 27th inst.	

26.9.19.

N. Neville Capt Major
for
Comdg 9th Bn Cheshire Regt.

WAR DIARY
or
INTELLIGENCE SUMMARY.

Army Form C. 2118.

9th Cheshire Vol 41

Place	Date	Hour	Summary of Events and Information	Remarks and references to Appendices
VILLERS L'HOPITAL.	Feby. 27th		Battalion in camp in VILLERS L'HOPITAL. Orders for move to Second Army Area postponed until 28th inst.	
	28th		Battalion embussed at 11;30 hours and entrained at CANDAS at 15.00 hours for ROISDORF (RHINE).	
			Lieut. M.M. THORBURN and 99 Other Ranks remained behind and were attached to 8/N. Staffordshire Regiment.	

Major,
Commanding 9th Bn Cheshire Regiment.

4/3/19.

www.ingramcontent.com/pod-product-compliance
Lightning Source LLC
Chambersburg PA
CBHW080853230426
43662CB00013B/2093